THE CHEFS' HEALTHY COLLECTION

THE CHEFS' HEALTHY COLLECTION

By Peggy Barnes

PELICAN PUBLISHING COMPANY
Gretna 1993

Library of Congress Cataloging-in-Publication Data

Barnes, Peggy.
  The chefs' healthy collection / by Peggy Barnes.
      p.   cm.
  Includes index.
  ISBN 0-88289-929-5
  1. Reducing diets.   I. Title.
RM222.2.B383   1993   92-30692
641.5'635—dc20   CIP

*The word "Pelican" and the depiction of a pelican are
trademarks of Pelican Publishing Company, Inc., and are
registered in the U.S. Patent and Trademark Office.*

Manufactured in the United States of America.

Published by Pelican Publishing Company, Inc.
1101 Monroe Street, Gretna, Louisiana 70053

This book is dedicated to my parents,
George and Margaret Walters, who, at their table,
taught me that from great love comes great food.

Contents

Acknowledgments

No venture of this distinction could have been completed without the efforts of a support team. I am pleased to have the opportunity to express my appreciation. First and foremost, my thanks go to the chefs who shared their recipes—especially Steven Hunn. For their creative vision and exact editing, I would like to thank Dana Bilbray, Nina Kooij, and Carolyn Ferrari.

Additionally, my thanks go to Mark Alexander for the sensational photography; Joseph Taylor for his elegant illustrations; Mary Ann Firth and Robin Cohen for their artful food styling; and Velynda Burnes, Marsha Vaught, Lauren Mueller, Dave Fagen, and Lisa Dellatorre for designing and organizing the completed art project.

I am grateful to Dottie Overman for her prompt, accurate answers to my culinary and nutritional questions; and to the Byliners, especially Joan Servis and Mary Lynn Dille, who kept me going.

Of course, to my wonderful, supportive husband, who has always been the best chef in my book, thank you!

A New Perspective

Seven years ago, while conducting an interview, I asked a well known chef what he recommended when a diner asked for something light. His eyebrows shot up to his toque. "Light? Bien sur! My roquefort cheese soufflé—it floats from the oven!"

"No, no," I said. "What about those of us who are trying to cut back on fat, eat more grains, you-are-what-you-eat sort of thing?"

"My dear," he bristled, "the reason people come to this restaurant is to indulge. Butter and cream is what they want! But if they insist, I send out some fish with a little lemon."

That was the attitude of yesterday. Today's diners are celebrating the good life in a bright new way. For the last three years, I have been collecting lower-calorie, lower-fat recipes from the country's top chefs—and most were eager to let me know that healthy cooking is the current trend in the restaurant business, and they were delighted to share their recipes.

Altogether, there are over 200 recipes from 77 chefs representing 44 cities and 72 restaurants. This book has become a compilation of the talents of many of the finest chefs in America today. Some chefs are as famous as the restaurants in which they work. You will find recipes from these multi-starred luminaries on our list alongside favorites from chefs without culinary medals on their chests. These are the talented people who are cooking up a healthy storm in the bistros and ethnic restaurants across the country. Many of today's epicureal artisans are young and cook with a vigor that is reflected in their cuisine. A surprisingly large number of them are women.

These chefs are unsurpassed in their imaginative use of fresh ingredients, proving that glorious eating can be an alliance of excitement and sensibility. I asked them for recipes containing less than 500 calories and not exceeding one tablespoon of oil per serving. Oh, what these experts can do with 500 healthy calories!! Many seem to believe that good food begins with the season's harvest, and they shared their secrets for elevating fruits and vegetables from dull to delectable. As you might expect, seafood was a popular subject, but the "fish with a little lemon" has been replaced with the likes of *Pan-Seared Swordfish with Toasted Rice Sauce.* Somewhat surprising to those who think low-fat eating does not include meat—pork, beef, veal, and lamb have been deliciously represented. Who could feel deprived eating *Lamb Spirals with Pine Nuts and Garlic?*

You will learn how the professionals cut the fat and up the flavor; how they concentrate seasonings for enlightened sauces; how they replace unhealthy frying with other techniques; how they use fresh herbs and vinegars to reduce sodium; and how they lower cholesterol while increasing the joy of cooking. In short, these recipes will show you how to eat with all your senses and create the most satisfying foods that you have ever served.

At last, there will be no need to compromise your low-caloried principles when entertaining. This collection is full of recipes to delight any guest—even those who have not quite jumped on the healthy bandwagon. An evening including *Peppered Tuna on Croutons, Garden Salad with Smoked Tomato Dressing, Tortelloni Kahala, and Orange Cloud Cake* could convert anyone.

Along with the recipes, you will find details on the restaurants of their origins, making this book a food lover's travel guide to healthy dining. While you are enjoying an evening at one of these great restaurants, perhaps you'll want to send for the chef to say hello to the artist whose recipes you have shared—-a fellow celebrant of our dynamic new way of dining.

To your health!

PEGGY BARNES

Featured Restaurants and Chefs

Adirondack's Denver, Colorado. Chef Gethin D. Thomas.
Cabernet Cassis Sauce (for Beef or Veal)

Antoine's New Orleans, Louisiana. Chef Bernard Guste.
Shrimp Ravigote

Ashley's at the Capital Little Rock, Arkansas. Chef Jeff Medbury.
Gruyère Cheese Soufflé

Barrow's House Dorset, Vermont.
Christmas Italian Rice Pudding
Portuguese Swordfish

Blue Strawbery Portsmouth, New Hampshire. Chef Phillip McGuire.
Italian Red Pepper Pesto.
Sautéed Shrimp with Radicchio on Apricot Brandy and Corn Relish
Tenderloin of Beef in a Gingered Brandy-Mustard Sauce
Tomatoes Stuffed with Eggplant and Potato Purée

Bon Ton Cafe New Orleans, Louisiana. Chef Wayne Pierce.
Crabmeat Imperial

Brasserie Savoy San Francisco, California. Chef Marc Meyer.
Rock Shrimp and Roast Corn Salad

By Word of Mouth Fort Lauderdale, Florida. Chef James Caron.
Pasta with Smoked Salmon and Dill

Cafe L'Europe Sarasota, Florida. Chef August Mrozowski.
Asparagus Bisque
Bouillabaisse
Champagne Melon Soup
Fillet of Sole Picasso
Florida Oysters Rockefeller
Mahimahi Oporto

California Cafe Corte Madera, California. Chef Michael Powers.
  Cappellini with Grilled Swordfish, Baby Vegetables, and Herb Broth

Casa Madrona Sausalito, California. Chef Kirke Byers.
  Sesame Beef with Asian Vinaigrette

Chef Allen's Miami, Florida. Chef Allen Susser.
  Key Lime Linquine with Crab and Pommery Mustard Sauce

Commander's Palace New Orleans, Louisiana. Chef Jamie Shannon.
  Baked Eggplant with Seafood
  Grilled Chicken with Tomato Pepper Salsa, Lemon-Caper Rice, and Asparagus
  Grilled Lamb with Vegetables, Rosemary Rice, and Balsamic Vinaigrette
  Baked Gulf Fish with Horseradish Crust

Court of Two Sisters New Orleans, Louisiana. Chef Peter Ferroe.
  Tuna Decatur

DC 3 Santa Monica, California. Chef William Hufferd.
  Lamb Spirals with Pine Nuts and Garlic

Domaine Chandon Napa Valley, California. Chef Philippe Jeanty.
  Roasted Vegetables Provençal
  Peppered Tuna on Croutons

Doral Saturnia International Miami, Florida. Chef Ron Hook.
  Chocolate Madeleines
  Sweet Corn and Clam Soup

Double's Club New York City. Chef Philip McGrath.
  Stonehill Chicken

Emiles San Jose, California. Chef Emile Mooser.
  Braised Veal Shanks
  Chicken with Mustard-Yogurt Sauce
  Roast Pork with Fruit Compote
  Roasted Pears with Bitter Chocolate Sorbet
  New Way Risotto

Everest Room Chicago, Illinois. Chef John Joho.
  Roasted Swordfish with Olives and Leeks

Faces Trattoria New York City.
  Grilled Chicken with Salad Greens and Fresh Herbs

Fio's La Fourchette St. Louis, Missouri. Chef Fio Antognini.
Belgian Endive and Orange Salad
Hawaiian Sorbet
Marinated Halibut Salad
Strawberry Grapefruit Soufflé
Veal Medallions in Creamy Chive Sauce

Four Seasons Philadelphia, Pennsylvania. Chef Jean-Marie Lacroix.
Pizza Provençal
Turkey Paillard with Cucumber Thai Salad
Pita with Mango and Avocado
Raspberry Mousse
Vegetable Salad with Truffle Dressing
Vegetable Consommé with Mushrooms.
Artichoke Ravioli with Tomato Compote

French Laundry Napa Valley, California. Chef Sally Schmitt.
Apricot Soufflé with Brandy Sauce
Winter Tomato Soup with Oregano and Orange

Gypsy Cab Company St. Augustine, Florida. Chef Nathan Pollack.
Grilled Salmon with Fresh Corn and Tomato Salsa

Halekulani Oahu, Hawaii. Chef George Mavrothalassitis.
Blackened Jumbo Scallops with Ferns and Watercress

Hamersley's Bistro Boston, Massachusetts. Chef Gordon Hamersley.
Garlic, Lemon, Olive, and Mint Compote for Pork or Lamb
Piri-Piri Vinaigrette for Grilled Steak
Spiced Lamb Shanks with Eggplant
Dry-Fried Shrimp with Roasted Shallots

Hedgerose Heights Inn Atlanta, Georgia. Chef Heinz Schwab.
Vegetable Terrine with Blue Cheese Mustard Sauce

Hunt Club Seattle, Washington. Chef Barbara Figueroa.
Sautéed Venison Medallions with Whidbey's Port Demi-Glace and Roasted Elephant Garlic

Iberian Huntington, New York. Chef Julio Villar.
Chicken Ajillo

Il Gattopardo New York City. Chef Mario Gattorna.
Pasta Primavera

Ivy's San Francisco. Chef Rick Cunningham.
Cornish Game Hen with Orange Apricot Sauce
Wild Rice Compote

Janos Tucson, Arizona. Chef Janos Wilder.
Salsa Fresca
Sea Scallops Sauté with Black Bean and Chipotle Stew
Sherried Black Bean Soup with Salsa Fresca

Joe's San Francisco, California.
Joe's Greek Special

John Clancy's New York City. Chef Melissa Lord.
Monkfish Medallions with Asparagus, Morels, and Madeira

Kahala Hilton Honolulu, Hawaii. Chef Dominique Jamain.
Poached Beef Filets on Fresh Horseradish Sauce
Tortelloni Kahala

King Cole Dayton, Ohio. Chef Steven Hunn.
Pasta with Goat Cheese, Tomato, and Cucumber
Roast Pork Tenderloin with Lemon Pear Chutney
Lentil, Red Pepper, and Onion Sauté
Oven-Baked Polenta
Wild Rice Cakes

Lafitte's Landing Donaldsonville, Louisiana. Chef John Folse.
Avocado Lafitte
Eggplant Creole
Shrimp Creole
Braised Redfish

Lark and The Dove Atlanta. Chef Michael Stanley.
Breast of Duck with Raspberry-Black Bean Gastrique

La Tour Chicago, Illinois. Chef Charles Weber.
Grilled Shrimp with Artichokes, Fettucini, and a Roasted Radicchio Vinaigrette
Smoked Venison Carpaccio with Hazelnuts, Currants, and Frisée

L'Auberge Dayton, Ohio. Chef Dieter Krug.
Chicken Breast with Morels
Asparagus Salad with Herb Dressing

Le Bernardin New York City. Chef Eberhard Müller.
Herb-Crusted Codfish in Rosemary Vinaigrette
Tropical Fruit Soup

Le Dome Fort Lauderdale, Florida.
  Jody's Fire and Ice Tomatoes

Mansion on Turtle Creek Dallas, Texas. Chef Dean Fearing.
  Pan-Seared Swordfish with Toasted Rice Sauce
  Broccoli-Pickled Eggplant Stir-Fry

Maisonette Cincinnati, Ohio. Chef Georges Haidon.
  Breast of Chicken Poached with Fresh Vegetables and Fine Herbs
  Floating Island on Strawberry Purée with Kiwi
  Veal Medallions with Braised Endives and Boiled Potatoes

Montrachet New York City. Chef Debra Ponzek.
  Coq au Riesling
  Soupe au Pistou

Nottoway Plantation White Castle, Louisiana. Chef Johnny Percle.
  Chef Johnny's Mardi Gras Vegetable Jambalaya

Occidental Washington, D.C.
  Pan-Seared Tuna Steak with Lobster and Fresh Fennel Sauce

Old Gin House St. Eustatius, Dutch Antilles.
  Caribbean Curried Soup

Opryland Nashville, Tennessee. Chef Richard Gerst.
  Garlic Salad Dressing

Palmier Bistro San Diego. Chef Jean-Pierre Martinez.
  Le Supreme de Poulet a la Provençale

Penelope's Restaurant Français Tucson, Arizona. Chef Patricia Sparks.
  Pears Poached in White Wine with Raspberry Sauce
  Poached Salmon with Dilled Cucumber Sauce

Peter's Indianapolis. Chef David Foegley.
  Cast Iron-Seared and Roasted Pheasant

Pompano Beach Club Bermuda.
  Bermuda Fish Chowder

Post House New York City. Chef Bob Mignola.
  Lemon Pepper Chicken

Printer's Row Chicago. Chef Michael Foley.
  Chicken with Raspberry Vinegar
  Roasted Yellow Pepper Soup with Basil

Ritz-Carlton Chicago, Illinois. Chef Pascal Vignau.
  Broiled Filet of Pacific Halibut with Cilantro Artichoke Relish
  Breast of Pheasant with Celery Root and Cranberry-Pepper Sauce
  Stove Top Pasta Salad

River Club Washington, D.C. Chef Jeff Tunks.
  Grilled Tuna on Roasted Vegetables with Pineapple-Soy Vinaigrette

Routh Street Cafe Dallas, Texas. Chef Stephan Pyles.
  Arugula and Fried Okra Salad with Roast Corn Vinaigrette
  Garden Salad with Smoked Tomato Dressing
  Golden Gazpacho with Bay Scallops
  Salmon Salad with Jicama and Papaya
  Vegetable Ragout
  Papaya-Serrano Chili Ice
  Red Snapper with Golden Tomato Salsa

Russian Tea Room New York City. Chef Anthony Damiano.
  Borscht
  Rigatoni with Apples and Bacon in a Peppered Vodka Sauce

Tack Room Tucson, Arizona. Chef David Lalli.
  Vino Gazpacho
  Mushroom Barley Soup

Topnotch Stowe, Vermont. Chef Louis Chevot.
  Butternut Squash Soup
  Orange Cloud Cakes with Boysenberry Sauce

Tree Top House Berkley, West Virginia. Chef Robert Siegworth.
  Crab-Papaya Veracruz
  Grilled Lobster and Scallop Kebobs
  Pecan Brown Rice

Trellis Cafe Williamsburg, Virginia. Chef Marcel Desaulniers.
  Sea Scallops with Scallions, Crispy Potatoes, and Lemon Dressing

Tribeca Grill New York City. Chef Don Pintabona.
  Sweet Corn Sauce for Seafood

Truffles at Casa Ybel Sanibel, Florida. Chef Mike Jacob.
  *Roasted Smoked Halibut with Braised Cabbage and Pars-
  leyed Potatoes*

Unicorn Village Miami, Florida. Chef Steven Petusevsky.
  *Udon Noodle, Shitake Mushrooms, and Green Onion Pan-
  cake with Peanut-Miso Sauce*
  Grilled Marinated Vegetable Cobb Salad
  Vegetable Sauté with Tuscan Spice Mix
  Mixed Berry and Granola Crisp

Upperline New Orleans, Louisiana. Chef Tom Cowman.
  Roasted Garlic
  Pasta with Sundried and Fresh Tomato Sauce

Van Dyke Place Detroit, Michigan. Chef Patrick Dunn.
  Apple Crackers
  Romaine Salad with Fresh Beet and Garlic Dressing
  Swordfish in Mustard Seed Crust

Wildflower Inn The Lodge at Vail, Colorado. Chef Jim Cohen.
  Salmon with Tomato and Chives

Yuca Coral Gables, Florida. Chef Douglas Rodriguez.
  Grilled Chicken with Honey, Lime, and Garlic Glaze
  Cuban Chicken Mojo
  Rice Primavera
  Gloria's Black Bean Soup

Zocalo Philadelphia, Pennsylvania. Chef Lou Sackett.
  Zocalo Black Beans
  Enchiladas Verdes

Additional Featured Chefs

Chef Lucy Chu
Pong Pong Chicken Salad
Chilled Chicken with Spicy Sauce
Poached Chicken
Chinese Stir-Fried Broccoli or Zucchini

Chef Robert Casella
Angel Hair Pasta with Chicken, Basil, and Olives
Ziti Italiano

Chef Robert Maxwell
Empanadas de Carne
Bangkok Pasta
Mango Mousse

Chef Paula Sideras
Brown and Wild Rice Salad

Chef Marian Stapleton
Crunchy Lunch
Chico's Chili

Appetizers
and
First Courses

Appetizers and First Courses

Avocado Lafitte

Florida Oysters Rockefeller

Sea Scallops with Scallions, Crispy Potatoes,
and Lemon Dressing

Apple Crackers

Salsa Fresca

Smoked Venison Carpaccio with Hazelnuts, Currants,
and Frisée

Sautéed Shrimp with Radicchio on Apricot Brandy
and Corn Relish

Vegetable Terrine with Blue Cheese Mustard Sauce

Grilled Shrimp with Artichokes, Fettucine, and
a Roasted Radicchio Vinaigrette

Pizza Provençal

Shrimp Ravigote

Empanadas de Carnes

Pita with Mango and Avocado

Peppered Tuna on Croutons

Gruyère Cheese Soufflé

Crab Papaya Veracruz

AVOCADO LAFITTE

As a first course or a luncheon salad, this delicately spiced filling of crab and Creole sauce provides a low-calorie answer to avocado cravings. The recipe is from Lafitte's Landing in Donaldsonville, Louisiana where John Folse was named National Chef of the Year.

4 Servings
Preparation Time: 25 minutes

2 ripe medium avocados, peeled
fresh lemon juice
4 tsp. low-fat mayonnaise
2 tsp. Creole mustard
4 chopped green onions
2 tbsp. white wine
2 tsp. Worcestershire sauce
dash hot pepper sauce
dash white pepper
8 oz. lump crabmeat
4 sprigs parsley
2 small papayas
8 strawberries, sliced in half
leaf lettuce
1 lemon, cut into wedges

1. Cut avocado in half, remove seed, and coat inside with lemon juice.

2. In a small mixing bowl, combine mayonnaise, mustard, green onion, wine, Worcestershire sauce, hot sauce, and white pepper. Fold in crabmeat.

3. Line each serving plate with leaf lettuce. Place avocado half in center of each plate. Top with crabmeat salad and a sprig of parsley.

4. Peel and seed papayas and slice lengthwise. Arrange papaya and strawberries around avocado. Garnish with lemon wedges.

ONE SERVING: 317 Calories; 14.6 grams Fat (2.6 Saturated); 35 mg Cholesterol.

FLORIDA OYSTERS ROCKEFELLER

Treasure the fast preparation time of this baked appetizer. It's from Chef August Mrozowski who always insists on the plumpest, freshest oysters for his patrons. August Mrozowski is executive chef at Cafe L'Europe, an eighteen-year tradition in Sarasota that is one of only two 4-star restaurants on the west coast of Florida.

4 Servings
Preparation Time: 15 minutes
Cooking Time: 10 minutes

24 raw oysters on the half shell
10 oz. fresh spinach, rinsed, dried, and finely chopped

¼ cup lemon juice
4 green onions, chopped
1 cup grated mozzarella cheese

1. Preheat oven to 400 degrees.

2. Place oysters (on their shells) in a baking pan. Top each oyster with a dab of spinach. Sprinkle with lemon juice, onions, and cheese. Bake at 400 degrees for 10 minutes.

ONE SERVING: 146 Calories; 7.3 grams Fat; 60 mg Cholesterol.

SEA SCALLOPS WITH JULIENNE OF SCALLIONS, CRISPY POTATOES, AND LEMON DRESSING

Glorious healthy food depends on texture and eye appeal as demonstrated in this lovely first course from The Trellis Cafe in Williamsburg, Virginia. Chef Marcel Desaulniers is on *Food and Wine* magazine's "Honor Roll of Chefs," and is the first chef from the southern United States to be named to the James Beard foundation.

HEALTH TIP: Six medium oysters contain only 58 calories and 46 milligrams of cholesterol. They are high in calcium, niacin, and iron and are good source of protein.

NOTE: The original recipe was supposedly named for John D. Rockefeller because it was so rich. This healthier version eschews butter and highlights the goodness of fresh, plump oysters. In most markets today, fresh oysters are available year-round. Refrigeration keeps them cool during hot weather, debunking the old myth of eating them during months spelled without an r. Generally, when selecting oysters, the smaller the oyster, the younger and more tender it will be.

VARIATION: This can serve four as a delightful luncheon salad. Use one medium potato for each potato circle. Top with shredded leaf lettuce, sautéed shrimp (or strips of smoked turkey breast), and the lemon dressing.

4 Servings
Cooking Time: 1 hour, 45 minutes + 40 minutes

2 large Idaho baking
  potatoes
3 tbsp. cider vinegar
3 tbsp. lemon juice
2 tsp. Dijon mustard
¾ cup plus 2 tbsp. olive
  oil
salt and freshly ground
  pepper

¾ lb. sea scallops, side
  muscle removed
1 large bunch watercress,
  stems removed,
  washed and dried
4 scallions, trimmed and
  cut into thin strips

1. Boil the whole, unpeeled potatoes for about 30 minutes in enough water to cover them. Remove and allow to cool for 1 hour under refrigeration.

2. To prepare lemon dressing, whisk together vinegar, 1½ tablespoons lemon juice, mustard, and salt and freshly ground pepper to taste. Continue to whisk the mixture while pouring in ¾ cup of olive oil in a slow, steady stream. Cover bowl with plastic wrap and set aside at room temperature until needed.

3. Preheat oven to 375 degrees. Peel potatoes and cut into slices about 1/16 inch thick.

4. Brush a baking sheet with 1 tablespoon of olive oil. On the baking sheet, make 4 circles of potatoes, allowing about half a potato for each portion. Each slice should slightly overlap the previous one, until a circle is formed. (At this point, the potatoes may be covered with plastic wrap and refrigerated for several hours).

5. Brush potatoes with remaining 1 tbsp. olive oil. Season with salt and pepper and bake in a 375-degree oven until golden brown, 20 to 25 minutes.

6. Reduce oven temperature to 150 degrees and keep crispy potatoes warm in the oven while searing scallops.

7. Season scallops with salt and pepper and remaining 1½ tablespoons lemon juice. Heat a non-stick sauté pan over medium heat. When the pan is hot, lightly brown scallops on both sides. Remove from skillet and slice into thin, julienne strips.

8. Using a spatula, place potato rings on serving plates. Arrange a spray of watercress in the center of each potato ring. Spoon 1 tablespoon of lemon dressing over watercress. Arrange scallop slices over watercress. Sprinkle scallion strips over scallops and serve immediately.

ONE SERVING: 317 Calories; 17.5 grams Fat (2.5 Saturated); 33 mg Cholesterol.

APPLE CRACKERS

These delightful morsels from Van Dyke Place in Detroit are so low in fat and calories that you can spread some wickedly rich cheese on top and still feel virtuous.

Makes 24 crackers
Preparation Time: 30 minutes
Cooking Time: 1 hour

10 medium Granny Smith
    apples, peeled, cored,
    and julienned
2 egg whites, beaten until
    they form soft peaks

cayenne pepper
black pepper
cheese for spreading

1. Preheat oven to 150 degrees.

2. Place apple strips on parchment paper on a baking sheet. Bake in a 150-degree oven for about 45 minutes, or until dry and crisp. Set apples aside; then increase oven temperature to 350 degrees.

3. Mix dried apple strips, beaten egg whites, and cayenne and black pepper to taste. Shape into thin wafers. Bake on a baking sheet at 350 degrees for 15 minutes, or until light golden brown. Serve with cheese.

ONE SERVING (Two crackers, without cheese): 70 Calories; 0.4 grams Fat; 0 mg Cholesterol.

NOTE: Using the parchment paper is important; the apples won't dry properly if placed directly on a baking pan.

NICE WITH: Richly flavorful cheeses, such as port wine cheddar or Stilton. With some scouting, you can find good-tasting low-fat cheeses.

HEALTH TIP: Freshly harvested apples not only taste better, but they differ in nutrients from those that have been stored for months. As apples sit in storage, their available carbohydrates increase, and calories increase along with them.

HINT: Janos says, "This salsa tastes best if served the same day it is made." Chilies are not only great for spicing up recipes, they are also a healthy addition to your diet. The recommended dietary allowance for vitamin A can be satisfied by eating about a teaspoon of red chili sauce, and one ounce of fresh green chilies—about two jalapenos—for vitamin C.

Here are some popular chilies ranking from mildest to hottest: Anaheim (green or red, tastes almost like a bell pepper); poblano (just a bit more pungent); ancho (dried poblanos); jalapeno, serrano (looks like small, thin jalapenos); Habanero ("from Havana"—the hottest chili in the world, known as the "Scotch bonnet" in the Caribbean).

SALSA FRESCA

Chef Janos Wilder serves this chunky salsa as a topping for his *Black Bean Soup*. You will find it equally valuable as an appetizer dip, perhaps served in a pottery bowl surrounded by wedges of healthy veggies and southwestern blue corn chips. Chef Wilder, one of James Beard's "Rising Stars in American Cuisine," reigns at his Mobil 4-Star restaurant, Janos, in Tucson, Arizona.

Makes 3 cups
Preparation Time: 20 minutes
Chill: At least 30 minutes

6 tomatoes, diced
½ cup finely diced red
   onions
1 bunch scallions, finely
   diced
1 Anaheim chili, peeled,
   seeded, and finely
   diced
½ poblano chili, peeled,
   seeded, and finely
   diced

1 bunch cilantro,
   coarsely chopped
1 tbsp. finely diced garlic
1 tbsp. balsamic vinegar
1 tbsp. red wine vinegar
1 tbsp. olive oil
salt and freshly ground
   pepper to taste

1. Combine all ingredients. Cover and chill.

ONE SERVING (¼ cup): 12 Calories; 1.3 grams Fat; 0 mg Cholesterol.

SMOKED VENISON CARPACCIO WITH HAZELNUTS, RED CURRANTS, AND FRISEE

Carpaccio is an appetizer of marinated, tender raw meat (usually beef), sliced paper-thin. This exotic version calls for an even leaner meat, venison, which is refrigerator-cured before smoking. Charles Weber is chef at La Tour in the Park-Hyatt Hotel in Chicago, Illinois.

4 Servings
Curing Time: 2 days
Preparation and Cooking Time: 1 hour

1½ lb. venison loin	½ pint red currants
2 tbsp. kosher salt	⅛ cup black currant
1½ tbsp. sugar	vinegar
3 tbsp. hazelnut oil	2 cups frisée lettuce, torn
½ cup chopped toasted	into bite-sized pieces
hazelnuts	

1. Sprinkle the venison loin with salt and sugar. Cover and refrigerate (to cure the meat) for 2 days.

2. Fire the smoker and when it is producing a lot of smoke, cut off heat to smoker. To smoke the cured venison, place venison in smoker and "cold smoke" it for about 20 minutes.

3. Remove venison from smoker, roll in plastic wrap, and place in freezer until it is firm enough to slice paper-thin.

4. Brush serving plates with 1 tablespoon of hazelnut oil. Slice the meat extra-thin and lay over entire surface of each plate.

5. Sprinkle hazelnuts over meat and garnish with currants.

6. Blend remaining 2 tablespoons oil with vinegar and toss with frisée. To serve, place a small mound of frisée salad in the center of each plate over the carpaccio.

ONE SERVING: 225 Calories; 13.6 grams Fat (1.1 Saturated); NA Cholesterol.

IN A HURRY? Purchase shelled and deveined shrimp and use thawed frozen corn.

SAUTEED SHRIMP WITH RADICCHIO ON APRICOT BRANDY AND CORN RELISH

This is one of the most frequently requested recipes from The Blue Strawbery in Portsmouth, New Hampshire. The Blue Strawbery (yes, there's just one "r" in "Strawbery") was chosen to be New Hampshire's best restaurant in numerous surveys.

4 Servings
Preparation Time: 25 minutes
Cooking Time: 10 minutes

3 large ears corn, husked and cleaned
½ tbsp. butter
1 clove garlic, crushed
1 cup chopped red bell pepper
¼ tsp. white wine vinegar

¼ cup apricot brandy
salt and pepper
1 lb. shrimp, shelled and cleaned
1 head radicchio, quartered

1. With a sharp knife, remove corn kernels from the cob.

2. In a skillet, melt the butter. Add garlic, corn, and red pepper; then sauté until corn is barely tender, about 3 minutes. Add vinegar, brandy, and salt and pepper to taste. Heat until steaming. Remove from heat and keep warm.

3. In the same skillet, sauté shrimp until they begin to turn pink, about 1 minute. Add radicchio and cook for 1 or 2 minutes more or until shrimp are done and radicchio is wilted. Do not overcook.

4. To serve, divide the corn relish between four plates, top with shrimp, and garnish with radicchio.

ONE SERVING: 254 Calories; 7.2 grams Fat (3.1 Saturated); 181 mg Cholesterol.

VEGETABLE TERRINE WITH BLUE CHEESE MUSTARD SAUCE

The diversity of vegetables is celebrated in this beautiful layered terrine from Heinz Schwab and his wife Penny, chefs and owners of The Hedgerose Heights Inn in Atlanta, Georgia. The restaurant was named one of Conde Naste's "Top Fifty Restaurants in America, and *Money* magazine's "Top Three Restaurants in Atlanta."

4 Servings
Preparation Time: 1 hour
Cooking Time: 1 hour
Chill: Overnight

10 oz. carrots, peeled and quartered lengthwise	2 tbsp. finely chopped parsley
10 oz. green beans, tips removed	2 tbsp. minced chives
10 oz. spinach, cleaned	2 tbsp. finely chopped tarragon
10 oz. cauliflower, cut into florets	salt and pepper
1½ oz. butter or margarine	ground nutmeg
1½ oz. all-purpose flour	4 oz. blue cheese
3 eggs	1 tbsp. mustard
5½ oz. low-fat milk	3 oz. low-fat mayonnaise
	1 oz. hot water
	lemon juice

1. In a large saucepan, bring salted water to boil. In separate batches, cook cauliflower, carrots, and spinach until tender. Plunge into cold water and drain.

2. Butter the inside of a terrine mold. Line with parchment paper and butter again.

3. In a bowl, combine flour and eggs and beat until completely incorporated. Add 4½ ounces of the milk, along with the parsley, chives, and tarragon. Adjust amount of herbs to taste and season with salt, pepper, and ground nutmeg.

4. Pour ⅓ of the batter into the mold to cover the bottom. Add the cauliflower, pressing well into the corners and bottom. Add green beans in a lengthwise layer; then add the carrots. Add ⅓ of the batter and top with the spinach. Press vegetables well into terrine; then add remaining batter.

NICE WITH: When the guests arrive, the host or hostess who serves this appetizer need only pour glasses of Chardonnay. To continue an evening of simple but sumptuous entertaining, have the grill ready for salmon steaks, zucchini halves, and corn-in-the-husk. Orange-vanilla frozen yogurt topped with fresh blueberries would make a delightful finale.

5. Cover with aluminum foil. Place terrine mold in a pan of water and cook in a 350-degree oven for 1 hour. Remove from oven and chill overnight in refrigerator.

6. Crumble the cheese into the food processor and add the mustard and remaining milk. Process until nearly smooth. Transfer contents into a mixing bowl and whisk in the mayonnaise, then the hot water. Season to taste with salt, pepper, and a few drops of lemon juice.

7. To unmold terrine, dip into warm water and turn onto serving plate. Serve with blue cheese mustard sauce.

ONE SERVING (Terrine): 232 Calories; 9.3 grams Fat (4.1 Saturated); 170 mg Cholesterol.

ONE SERVING (Sauce): 150 Calories; 11.6 grams Fat (6.2 Saturated); 27 mg Cholesterol.

HEALTH TIP: Shallots have only about seven calories per tablespoon.

GRILLED SHRIMP WITH ARTICHOKE HEARTS, FETTUCINE, AND A ROASTED RADICCHIO VINAIGRETTE

Radicchio roasted on a charcoal grill, tossed with balsamic vinegar, herbs, grilled shrimp, and a little pasta creates a spectacular nineties-style first course! Charles Weber creates menu magic at La Tour restaurant in Chicago's Park-Hyatt Hotel.

4 Servings
Marinate: At least 2 hours
Cooking Time: 25 minutes

½ cup balsamic vinegar
1 cup olive oil
2 tbsp. minced shallot
2 tbsp. minced garlic
4 tbsp. fresh basil
4 tbsp. fresh lemon juice

1 head radicchio
24 shrimp, peeled and deveined
½ lb. fettucine
artichoke hearts
basil leaves

1. Heat water for pasta. Preheat grill.

2. Combine first six ingredients and blend well.

3. Without removing the core from the radicchio, cut it into quarters and marinate in the vinaigrette for at least 2 hours.

4. Squeeze the vinaigrette out of the radicchio, reserving vinaigrette. Grill the radicchio over medium-hot coals until it softens, 4 to 5 minutes. Remove core and purée radicchio with the vinaigrette in a blender until smooth.

5. Cook fettucine according to package directions. Drain.

6. Grill shrimp just until tender. Toss with the fettucine and vinaigrette. Accompany the dish with artichoke hearts and garnish with basil leaves.

ONE SERVING: 245 Calories; 15.0 grams Fat (2.1 Saturated); 60 mg Cholesterol.

PIZZA PROVENÇAL

Americans eat 90 acres of pizza per day—mostly loaded with high-fat toppings. Health-conscious pizza lovers will treasure this enlightened version from Chef Jean-Marie Lacroix. Delicious, healthy choices of "Alternate Cuisine" are always on the menu at the Four Seasons resort in Philadelphia.

4 Servings
Preparation Time: 10 minutes
Cooking Time: 7 minutes

1 10-inch pre-baked pizza
   crust
1 oz. Dijon mustard
2 large, ripe tomatoes,
   thinly sliced
salt and freshly ground
   pepper

4 oz. goat cheese (plain,
   or herb-garlic
   flavored)
4 tbsp. shredded fresh
   basil leaves
4 tsp. olive oil

HINT: Have you tried using boboli (bo'-bo-lee)? Found in most grocery stores, boboli are baked pizza crusts that have been spiked with part-skim mozzarella, olive oil, and parmesan cheese. The four-ounce size has three hundred calories, seven grams of fat, and six hundred milligrams of sodium.

1. Preheat oven to 500 degrees.

2. Paint pizza crust with a light coating of mustard. Arrange tomatoes on top of mustard. Season with salt and pepper.

3. Crumble goat cheese on top of tomatoes. Sprinkle basil on top and drizzle olive oil over all. Bake at 500 degrees for 7 minutes. Slice into eight wedges.

ONE SERVING (Two slices): 310 Calories; 10.6 grams Fat (3.4 Saturated); 86 mg Cholesterol.

SHRIMP RAVIGOTE

This is an extravagant beginning to any meal. The anchovies speak softly in this quick-to-the-table New Orleans shrimp fest. *Louisiana Life* readers chose Antoine's in New Orleans as the best Creole restaurant in Louisiana. Seafood recipes, like this one from chef Bernard Guste, have delighted diners at Antoine's for 150 years.

6 Servings
Preparation Time: 10 minutes (using precooked shrimp)

½ cup minced green bell pepper
4 anchovy filets, minced
8 oz. low-calorie mayonnaise
3 green onions, minced
2 tbsp. minced pimento

1½ lb. boiled and peeled shrimp
watercress
tomato wedges
6 anchovy filets for garnish

1. Mix together the first five ingredients. Gently fold in the shrimp.

2. Place on a bed of watercress and garnish with tomato wedges and anchovy filets.

ONE SERVING: 298 Calories; 7.4 grams Fat (Saturated 0.5); 226 mg Cholesterol.

HINT: Rinse canned anchovies with cold water and pat dry to remove oil.

NICE WITH: Mesquite-grilled beef, pan-seared potatoes, and a simple green salad.

EMPANADAS DE CARNES

These are savory meat pies with a Spanish heritage from a chef who serves them at sunset in the cockpits of luxurious charter yachts. Robert Maxwell, after working as a chef at top restaurants in Florida, now prepares elaborate gourmet meals on charter yachts in the Caribbean. His guests often request low-calorie dishes. "Today's men and women want to stay in shape, even on vacation," Maxwell says, "They don't leave their principles of healthy eating at home."

Makes 24 appetizers
Preparation Time: 1 hour
Cooking Time: 25 minutes

2 cups all-purpose flour	1 small ripe tomato, diced
⅓ cup plus 1 tbsp. olive oil	¼ cup currants
⅓ cup warm water	¼ cup chopped green olives
1 tsp. plus 1 tbsp. sherry vinegar	½ tsp. dried oregano
1¼ tsp. salt	½ tsp. paprika
¼ cup minced green or yellow bell pepper	½ tsp. ground cumin
½ cup finely chopped onion	¼ tsp. hot pepper sauce
¾ lb. very lean ground beef	1 egg
	1 tbsp. cold water
	spray cooking oil

1. Preheat oven to 350 degrees.

2. In a mixing bowl stir flour, ⅓ cup oil, warm water, 1 teaspoon vinegar, and 1 teaspoon salt until dough comes together. Gather into a ball and knead gently until smooth. Let rest, loosely covered, for 30 minutes.

3. Meanwhile, in a large skillet heat remaining tablespoon olive oil. Add pepper and onions and sauté over medium heat until onions are golden, 2 to 3 minutes. Add beef and cook, breaking up meat, until beef is no longer pink, 3 to 5 minutes. Stir in tomato, currants, olives, remaining tablespoon vinegar, oregano, paprika, ¼ teaspoon salt, ground cumin, and hot pepper sauce. Cook, stirring constantly, for 2 minutes. Remove from heat and let cool.

IN A HURRY? Instead of preparing the dough, substitute prepared refrigerated pie dough or biscuits from your market's dairy case. Roll out circles and continue with directions for filling, brushing with egg wash, and baking. (Baking time may be slightly reduced.

4. Spray 2 baking sheets with spray cooking oil. Beat together the egg and 1 tablespoon cold water to make an egg wash.

5. Cut dough into 24 pieces. On a lightly floured surface, roll out each piece to a 4-inch circle. Place a rounded tbsp. of filling on center of circle. Brush inside edges with egg wash, fold circle in half and press edges together with a fork. Repeat with remaining dough and filling. Brush tops with egg wash and bake at 350 degrees for 15 minutes; then turn and continue baking for 5 to 10 minutes, or until golden brown. Serve hot or at room temperature.

ONE SERVING (One Empanada): 105 Calories; 8.4 grams Fat; 69 mg Cholesterol.

HEALTH TIP: Try using one of the bottled no-oil vinaigrette dressings.

WHOLE WHEAT PITA WITH MANGO AND AVOCADO

Enjoy this sandwich that's up on flavor and down on calories, fat, and cholesterol. At the Four Seasons restaurant in Philadelphia, Chef Jean-Marie Lacroix features eclectic cuisine using only the freshest ingredients, including locally-grown produce.

4 Servings
Preparation Time: 10 minutes

2 whole wheat pita bread slices
red leaf lettuce
1 cup peeled and diced mango
1 cup peeled and diced avocado
2 tsp. lemon juice
2 tbsp. low-calorie vinaigrette
2 tbsp. chopped basil
2 tomatoes, peeled, seeded, and diced
salt and pepper to taste

1. Cut each pita in half. Line with lettuce.

2. Combine remaining ingredients and stuff inside pita pockets.

ONE SERVING: 105 Calories; 6.1 grams Fat (.9 Saturated); 0 mg Cholesterol.

PEPPERED TUNA ON CROUTONS

These herb-scented tuna treats will become a favorite for entertaining, but your guests will probably be too busy raving about the taste to appreciate the low fat and cholesterol counts. Phillipe Jeanty is executive chef of the restaurant at Domaine Chandon, the winery in Yountville, California. Because Domaine Chandon bottles some of the best sparkling wines in the world, it is not surprising that he suggests accompanying these tidbits with a glass of champagne.

Makes 25 appetizers
Preparation Time: 45 minutes

1 lb. fresh yellowfin tuna
2 tbsp. olive oil
freshly ground black
    pepper
1 red sweet pepper,
    roasted, seeded,
    skinned, and diced
1 tbsp. chopped parsley

1 tbsp. chopped fresh
    tarragon (or 1 tsp.
    dried)
1 large garlic clove,
    crushed
1 tbsp. lemon juice
salt to taste
1 baguette loaf
olive oil

1. Preheat grill or sauté pan.

2. Rub tuna with 1 tablespoon olive oil. Coat with pepper. Grill to medium rare or sauté over medium-high heat. Cool.

3. Discard the skin and bones, then flake the tuna into a bowl. Add red pepper, parsley, tarragon, garlic, lemon juice, and 1 tablespoon olive oil. Mix lightly. Taste for seasoning. You may choose to add more lemon, salt, or a bit more oil.

4. Cut thin slices from the baguette. Brush lightly with olive oil and toast until brown.

5. Spread tuna mixture on croutons and serve.

ONE SERVING (Two Croutons): 148 Calories; 4.6 grams Fat; 5 mg Cholesterol.

NOTE: One method of roasting peppers is to cut them in half, place them on a baking sheet in a 425-degree oven for about 30 minutes, or until the skin is blackened. Remove from the oven and place in a bowl, cover with plastic wrap, and let them sit for about 15 minutes. Then you can easily peel off the skin and chop the peppers.

IN A HURRY? Substitute prepared roasted peppers from a jar or sautéed fresh chopped red peppers.

VARIATION: Try sprinkling Creole seasoning on the croutons after brushing with olive oil and toasting.

VARIATION: To further reduce the cholesterol in this dish, replace the eggs with an egg substitute product. That version, although not puffy like a soufflé, will have the appearance and texture of an omelet.

NICE WITH: As a side dish, the soufflé (or the omelet variation) is delicious with a lean ham steak and lightly sautéed onions and peppers.

NOTE: The classic soufflé dish is a round, oven-proof dish with straight sides that facilitate the soufflé's rising. A variety of sizes are available in most kitchenware shops.

GRUYERE CHEESE SOUFFLE

As light as a whisper, this soufflé would make a delightful opening to a memorable dinner party, or it can be given top billing as a luncheon dish. Ashley's At The Capital Hotel, where Jeff Medbury is the chef, is in Little Rock, Arkansas.

4 Servings
Preparation and Cooking Time: 1½ hours

butter
2 tbsp. grated parmesan cheese
1½ cups skim milk
3 tbsp. whole wheat flour
1 cup grated Gruyère cheese (4 oz.)

1 cup grated mild cheddar cheese (4 oz.)
5 eggs, separated
¼ tsp. cayenne pepper
¼ tsp. cream of tartar

1. Preheat oven to 350 degrees.

2. Lightly butter an 8-cup soufflé dish and sprinkle parmesan cheese on bottom and sides of bowl.

3. In a saucepan, heat 1 cup of the skim milk until simmering. In a small bowl, whisk together the remaining ½ cup skim milk and flour. Add to the saucepan, stirring constantly, until mixture thickens; then remove from heat.

4. Add Gruyère, cheddar, and cayenne. Add egg yolks as soon as the mixture is cool enough to avoid cooking them. Mix thoroughly to obtain a smooth, lump-free sauce.

5. In a mixing bowl, beat the egg white until foamy. Add cream of tartar and continue beating until egg whites are stiff and hold their shape, but still have a velvety appearance.

6. Fold cheese mixture into egg whites.

7. Pour mixture into the prepared soufflé bowl. Place in a pan of water and bake at 350 degrees for 1 hour and 15 minutes, or until set. Serve immediately.

ONE SERVING: 340 Calories; 24.4 grams Fat (13.2 Saturated); 359 mg Cholesterol.

CRAB PAPAYA VERACRUZ

The delicate flavor of crab is enlivened with sautéed vegetables in this low-calorie specialty of Chef Robert Siegworth of Tree Top House in Berkley, West Virginia.

6 Servings
Preparation Time: 25 minutes

3 small ripe papayas
curly-leaf lettuce leaves
vegetable cooking spray
1 tsp. unsalted margarine
¼ cup chopped green onion
¼ cup chopped green pepper
¼ cup chopped red pepper

2 medium tomatoes, seeded and chopped
¼ cup spicy vegetable cocktail juice
1 tbsp. fresh lime juice
1 tbsp. chopped fresh cilantro
½ tsp. dried oregano
¾ lb. fresh jumbo lump crabmeat, drained and flaked

1. Cut papayas in half lengthwise; scoop out and discard seeds. Place papaya halves, cut side up, on a lettuce-lined platter.

2. Coat a large, non-stick skillet with cooking spray. Add margarine. Place over medium heat until hot. Add onions and peppers, and sauté for 3 to 4 minutes, or until tender. Add tomatoes and next 4 ingredients. Cook for 2 minutes. Add crabmeat, stirring well until heated.

3. To serve, use a slotted spoon to mound crabmeat mixture into each papaya half.

ONE SERVING: 155 Calories; 1.8 grams Fat (0.3 Saturated); 58 mg Cholesterol.

HEALTH TIP: Papaya supplies hefty amounts of vitamin C, beta-carotene, and vitamin A. The fruit also contains papain, a digestive enzyme.

MAKE AHEAD: The crab filling may be made up to two hours in advance. Refrigerate until ready to serve, then reheat filling in a microwave oven on medium power for one minute. Resume recipe at Step Three.

Soups

Soups

Roasted Yellow Pepper Soup with Basil
Sherried Black Bean Soup with Salsa Fresca
Bermuda Fish Chowder
Vegetable Consommé with Mushrooms
Sweet Corn and Clam Soup
Asparagus Bisque
Bouillabaisse
Winter Tomato Soup with Oregano and Orange
Champagne Melon Soup
Montrachet's Soupe au Pistou
Vino Gazpacho
Gloria's Black Bean Soup
Tropical Fruit Soup
Golden Gazpacho with Bay Scallops
Butternut Squash Soup
Mushroom Barley Soup
Caribbean Curried Soup
The Russian Tea Room Borscht

ROASTED YELLOW PEPPER SOUP WITH BASIL

No collection of recipes from great chefs could exclude Michael Foley whose low-calorie creations are savored at Printer's Row in Chicago. Sample his artistry in this colorful soup which may be served hot or chilled.

6 Servings
Preparation Time: 1 hour

6 whole yellow peppers	**1 qt. vegetable stock**
1 whole red pepper	**½ cup plain low-fat**
olive oil	**yogurt, whisked well**
4 unpeeled whole	**10 fresh basil leaves,**
shallots	**sliced thin**

1. Preheat oven to 400 degrees.

2. Rub peppers with olive oil, then roast on a flat baking pan in the preheated oven for 30 minutes, turning every 10 minutes until well charred.

3. Meanwhile, in another baking pan, roast shallots the same way, but without olive oil, for 30 minutes.

4. Clean the charred skin off both the red and yellow peppers, remove seeds and chop fine, keeping the red pepper separate. Place red pepper in a blender and purée until smooth.

5. Peel roasted shallots and chop fine.

6. In a large saucepan, bring vegetable stock to a boil. Lower heat to medium, add the chopped shallots and roasted yellow pepper. Let simmer for 5 minutes. Remove from heat and place half the mixture in a blender container and purée until smooth. Purée the other half, then return mixture to saucepan (see *Hint*). Stir in yogurt.

7. Ladle soup into bowls and garnish each with 1 tablespoon red pepper purée and sliced basil OR chill and garnish at serving time.

ONE SERVING: 50 Calories; 1 gram Fat; 7 mg Cholesterol.

HINT: If you choose to serve the soup warm, be sure that it is not too hot when yogurt is added; otherwise, the yogurt will curdle.

HEALTH TIP: To prepare a low-fat, nourishing vegetable stock, use a variety of veggies and simmer in twice as much liquid as vegetables. Browning the vegetables first is optional. Try using tomatoes, lettuce, parsnips, leeks, green pea pods, carrots, onions, and a variety of herbs and spices. Cook until vegetables are tender; then strain.

SHERRIED BLACK BEAN SOUP WITH SALSA FRESCA

From Chef Janos Wilder's Mobil 4-Star restaurant, Janos, in Tucson, Arizona, this simple combination of a few ingredients creates rich satisfaction. While this soup is simmering, the aroma from the kitchen will drive you mad!

6 Servings
Preparation Time: overnight
Cooking Time: 4½ hours

olive oil
1 yellow onion, coarsely chopped
2 carrots, coarsely chopped
3 tbsp. chopped garlic
salt
freshly ground pepper to taste

1¼ cups (10 oz.) dried black beans, picked over and soaked overnight
3 cups chicken stock
4 oz. grated parmesan cheese
½ cup dry sherry
4 tbsp. Jano's Salsa Fresca (see index)

1. Coat the bottom of a soup pot with olive oil. Add onions, carrots, garlic, salt, and pepper. Sauté until the onions are translucent.

2. Drain and rinse the beans. Add beans and stock to soup pot and bring to a boil. Cover and cook until beans are quite soft, about 4 hours. As soup simmers, you may have to add water to replace liquid lost to evaporation. The completed soup should be quite thick.

3. Just before serving, stir in cheese and sherry. Serve in soup bowls garnished with Jano's Salsa Fresca.

ONE SERVING (Without Salsa Fresca): 191 Calories; 5.1 grams Fat (2.0 Saturated); 14 mg Cholesterol.

HEALTH TIP: One cup of beans provides 15 grams of protein (roughly a quarter of the Recommended Daily Allowance), about 200 calories, and only a single gram of fat.

BERMUDA FISH CHOWDER

After sampling this specialty soup of The Pompano Beach Club in Bermuda, visitors often leave the island with souvenir bottles of the local sherry pepper hot sauce that is served on the side.

8 Servings
Preparation Time: 20 minutes
Cooking Time: 50 minutes

2 tbsp. vegetable oil
3 celery stalks, chopped
2 medium carrots, chopped
1 large onion, chopped
1 medium green bell pepper, chopped
3 garlic cloves, finely chopped
3 tbsp. tomato paste
4 cups fish stock or bottled clam juice
2 large russet potatoes, peeled, cut into ½-inch dice

1 16-oz. can tomatoes, chopped, juices reserved
2 tbsp. Worcestershire sauce
1 large jalapeno chili, minced with seeds
1 tsp. dried thyme, crumbled
1 bay leaf
1 lb. red snapper filets, cut into ½-inch pieces
salt and freshly ground pepper

1. In a large, heavy pot, heat oil over medium heat. Add celery, carrots, onion, pepper and garlic. Sauté until all vegetables are tender, about 8 minutes. Stir in tomato paste and cook for 1 minute. Add stock, potatoes, tomatoes, tomato juice, Worcestershire sauce, jalapenos, thyme, and bay leaf. Simmer until potatoes are tender, stirring occasionally for about 30 minutes.

2. Add red snapper; then cover and simmer until snapper is just cooked through, about 10 minutes. Season soup to taste with salt and pepper. Ladle soup into bowls and serve.

ONE SERVING: 249 Calories; 8.8 grams Fat (1.7 Saturated); 41 mg Cholesterol.

VEGETABLE CONSOMME
WITH MUSHROOMS

A soup-most-fragrant with aromatic vegetables and earthy mushrooms is from the Fountain restaurant at the Four Seasons Resort in Philadelphia, which has received numerous awards as a result of the talents of executive chef, Jean-Marie Lacroix.

6 Servings
Preparation Time: 50 minutes

2 tbsp. plus 1 tsp. virgin
    olive oil
1 leek (white part only),
    cut in half lengthwise
1 large onion, coarsely
    chopped
2 ribs celery, coarsely
    chopped
2 carrots, coarsely
    chopped
2 cloves garlic, peeled
3 shallots, chopped
½ bunch fresh parsley (or
    2 tbsp. dried)

½ bunch fresh basil (or
    2 tbsp. dried)
6 white mushrooms,
    chopped
7 tomatoes, coarsely
    chopped
2½ qt. water
6 wild mushrooms,
    chopped
2 ribs celery, blanched
    1 minute and
    chopped
1 carrot, blanched
    2 minutes and
    chopped

1. Heat 2 tbsp. olive oil in a large pot. Add all ingredients up to, but not including, the water. Sauté for 5 minutes, until onions are translucent. Add the water, cover, and cook over low heat until water is reduced by half, about 30 minutes. Strain through a fine strainer.

2. Sauté the chopped wild mushrooms in 1 teaspoon olive oil for 3 minutes, until crispy. Drain well on paper towel.

3. To serve, place hot consommé into soup bowls. Top with mushrooms and blanched celery and carrots.

ONE SERVING: 90 Calories; 5.1 grams Fat (0.7 Saturated); 0 mg Cholesterol.

HEALTH TIP: Studies have shown that dieters who start their meals with a light soup, such as this one, tend to consume fewer total calories and lose weight faster.

MAKE AHEAD: The soup
can be prepared in ad-
vance through Step 3.
Cover and refrigerate.
Bring to room temperature
before resuming recipe.

HEALTH TIP: Evaporated
skim milk can substitute
for forbidden cream in
many recipes; it has a
skinny 25 calories per
ounce, with no saturated
fat.

IN A HURRY?: Use frozen
corn and ask your sea-
food market for fresh
chopped clams.

SWEET CORN AND CLAM SOUP

Ron Hook, chef at the Doral Saturnia International Spa Resort in Miami, says, "For the freshest ingredients, I rely on
my own herb garden and a small, but expanding organic
vegetable garden." Here he purées fresh corn to add a subtle
sweetness and creamy consistency to this soup.

Makes 4 cups
Preparation Time: 20 minutes
Cooking Time: 1 hour, 15 minutes

**7 to 8 medium ears fresh
corn
4 cups chicken stock or
canned low-sodium
broth
½ cup bottled clam juice
12 freshly shucked
littleneck clams,
clams chopped and
liquid reserved**

**½ cup canned evaporated
skim milk
freshly ground pepper
minced chives for garnish**

1. Shuck the corn. Using a thin, sharp knife and working
over a large bowl, cut the kernels from the ears of corn,
scraping the cobs with the knife to extract any juices. You
should have 4 cups of corn. Reserve the cobs.

2. In a medium, flameproof casserole, combine the corn and
the cobs with the chicken stock, clam juice, reserved fresh
clam liquid, and evaporated milk. Cook over moderate heat
for 45 minutes.

3. Remove and discard the cobs. In a blender, purée the
soup in 2 batches until fairly smooth. Strain into a medium
saucepan.

4. Bring the soup to a boil over moderately high heat. Stir in
the chopped clams, cook for 30 seconds, then remove from
heat. Season to taste with pepper. Pour the soup into shallow bowls and garnish with the chives.

ONE SERVING: 264 Calories; 3.9 grams Fat (0.8 Saturated); 13 mg Cholesterol.

ASPARAGUS BISQUE

Somehow, the low-calorie, low-fat ingredients that are blended with fresh asparagus in this delicious soup come out tasting like butter and cream. At Cafe l'Europe in Sarasota, Florida, diners can always make healthy choices. Chef August Mrozowski offers a daily complete menu that has been approved by the American Heart Association.

6 Servings
Preparation and Cooking Time: 40 minutes

1 cup low-sodium chicken broth	2 cups skim milk
1 tbsp. low-calorie margarine	2 tbsp. cornstarch
2 cups fresh asparagus, trimmed and sliced	2 tbsp. water
1 clove garlic, minced	1 tbsp. white wine
	dash white pepper
	salt (optional)

1. In a large saucepan, combine chicken broth and margarine and bring to a boil. Add asparagus and garlic. Reduce heat, cover, and simmer for 10 minutes or until the asparagus is tender. Remove from heat. Do not drain.

2. In a small saucepan over low heat, heat the skim milk. In a small bowl, combine the cornstarch with 2 tablespoons water, and stir until smooth. Add the cornstarch mixture to the milk, stirring constantly to prevent lumping. When the mixture has thickened, remove from heat and allow to cool.

3. In a blender or food processor, combine asparagus and broth mixture with the thickened white sauce. Add the white wine. Blend until smooth. Taste for seasoning, adding pepper and salt if desired. Serve warm, reheating slightly over low heat if necessary.

ONE SERVING: 46 Calories; 1.0 grams Fat; 1.0 mg Cholesterol.

VARIATION: Bouillabaisse begs for variations on the types of fish and seafood used—it is actually more of a general category than a particular recipe. In a ballad by Thackery, bouillabaisse was immortalized as "a noble dish—a sort of soup, or broth or brew."

BOUILLABAISSE

Legend has it that bouillabaisse was divinely inspired, brought by angels to shipwrecked early Christians on a Mediterranean island. This version is brought to us from Chef August Mrozowski at Cafe L'Europe in Sarasota.

10 Servings
Preparation Time: 25 minutes
Cooking Time: 45 minutes

2 tbsp. olive oil
1 cup chopped carrots
1 large garlic bulb, peeled and chopped
1 cup chopped red onion
1 leek, white part only, chopped
2 tbsp. chopped fresh oregano
1 tbsp. fennel seed
1 cup chopped celery
1 cup chopped fresh fennel bulb
1 lb. tomatoes, peeled, seeded, and cut into large chunks

½ tsp. saffron (or more to taste)
1 bay leaf
2 qt. fish broth or bottled clam juice
12 shrimp with shells (20-30 count)
12 littleneck clams
12 oz. lobster meat
1 lb. fish (snapper, grouper, mahimahi, salmon), cut into 10 pieces
½ tsp. white pepper
salt to taste

1. In a large pot, heat oil then add carrots, garlic, onion, and leeks and sauté for 1 minute. Add oregano, fennel seed, celery, fresh fennel, tomatoes, saffron, bay leaf, and fish broth. Bring to a boil; then reduce heat and simmer for about 30 minutes.

2. Add shrimp, clams, lobster, and fish. Cook over medium-high heat for another 4 to 5 minutes, or until fish is just cooked through. Reduce heat, add white pepper and salt to taste, and serve.

ONE SERVING: 205 Calories; 1.5 grams Fat; 96 mg Cholesterol.

WINTER TOMATO SOUP
WITH OREGANO AND ORANGE

This soup has a Mexican theme, and it should be no surprise that chefs often look south of the border for inspiration. Mexican, along with Chinese and French cooking are thought to be the only three truly original cuisines of the world. Sally Schmitt is one of many talented chefs who migrated to Napa Valley and changed the way the world felt about American cooking. She and her husband oversee the charming restaurant called The French Laundry in Yountville, California.

Makes: 8 cups
Preparation and Cooking Time: 30 minutes

1 28-oz.can tomatoes,
    drained, reserve juice
4 corn tortillas
2 tsp. olive oil
1 medium onion, thinly
    sliced
2 cloves garlic, thinly
    sliced
½ cup thinly sliced
    tomatillos
½ cup yellow tomato
    cubes

½ cup red tomato cubes
1 46-oz. can chicken
    broth
zest of one orange
juice of one orange
    (about ½ cup)
salt and pepper
2 tbsp. chopped fresh
    oregano
½ cup low-fat yogurt
    mixed with 1 tbsp.
    ground cumin

1. In a food processor or blender, briefly chop the canned tomatoes.

2. In a heavy-bottomed soup pot, over high heat, crisp the tortillas by cooking on each side until they puff up and start to turn brown. Cut into strips and set aside.

3. In the same pot, heat olive oil, then add the onion and garlic and sauté over medium-low heat until onions are translucent, about 3 minutes. Add tomatillos and fresh tomato cubes and sauté until hot.

4. Add chopped canned tomatoes, reserved tomato juice, chicken broth, orange zest, and orange juice. Taste for seasoning; add salt and pepper if needed. Add oregano and bring to a simmer.

HINT: When selecting canned tomatoes, many cooks prefer Italian plum tomatoes because their flavor is rich enough to stand up to the canning process. In the winter, when other varieties of fresh tomatoes are drab and tasteless, fresh Italian tomatoes can be used reliably for cooking. All tomatoes that are not yet ripe should be ripened at room temperature in a brown paper bag.

HEALTH TIP: Tomatillos, little Mexican green tomatoes with papery husks, belong to the same botanical family as red, globe tomatoes, and are just as rich in vitamins A and C. Choose firm fruit with dry, tight-fitting husks; remove husks and wash fruit before slicing, eating, or cooking.

5. Garnish with tortilla strips and a dollop of the yogurt-cumin mixture.

ONE SERVING: 185 Calories; 4.7 grams Fat; 1 mg Cholesterol.

HINT: Chill the dishes as well as the soup in the refrigerator all day or overnight. Adjust seasonings after chilling.

CHAMPAGNE MELON SOUP

Much more than the sum of its fruits, this elegant, warm-weather soup is another from Cafe L'Europe.

6 Servings
Preparation Time: 15 minutes
Chilling Time: 30 minutes

2 cups chopped
   cantaloupe
2 cups chopped
   honeydew melon
½ cup freshly squeezed
   orange juice

1 tbsp. freshly squeezed
   lemon juice
1 tbsp. freshly squeezed
   lime juice
½ cup chilled champagne
mint leaves for garnish
(optional)

1. In a blender, purée melon and fruit juices. Chill for at least 30 minutes. Add champagne and serve garnished with mint leaves, if desired.

ONE SERVING: 60 Calories; 0 grams Fat; 0 mg Cholesterol.

NOTE: The French term, pistou (pees-too), has two definitions. One is the blend of basil, garlic, and olive oil that is called pesto in Italy. Pistou also refers to a French soup made of beans, onions, tomatoes, and pasta that is seasoned with the basil-garlic mix.

MONTRACHET'S SOUPE AU PISTOU

Regarding the stylish New York City restaurant, Montrachet, and its famous chef, Gourmet magazine says, "Debra Ponzek's style of cooking is light at all times. She likes to go with the provençal summertime custom of preparing soupe au pistou with white beans, garlic, and basil."

4-6 Servings
Preparation Time: 20 minutes (does not include soaking
  time for beans)
Cooking Time: 1½ hours

2 tbsp. finely chopped
  garlic
1 tbsp. olive oil
¼ cup fresh fava or lima
  beans
½ cup great northern
  white beans,
  presoaked
10 cups chicken stock
1 cup finely chopped
  zucchini
1 cup finely chopped
  yellow squash
½ cup skinless, seedless
  tomatoes
1 cup finely chopped
  carrots

½ cup chopped leeks,
  white part only
salt and pepper
cooked pasta (optional
  ¼ cup per serving)

Pistou:
1 cup cleaned basil leaves
½ cup extra virgin olive
  oil
⅛ cups pine nuts
⅛ cup parmesan cheese
2 cloves garlic, peeled
  and lightly mashed
1 tsp. salt
¼ tsp. pepper

MAKE AHEAD: This soup can be made ahead of time and reheated. It also freezes beautifully—but don't add pasta until just before serving.

1. In a large, heavy pan, sauté garlic in olive oil. Add beans and cover with stock. Cook until beans are tender, 30 to 40 minutes. Add remaining vegetables and cook until tender, about 30 minutes. Season to taste with salt and pepper.

2. Using a food processor or blender, grind the pistou (pesto) ingredients to a smooth paste. Do not over-process or the basil will become too dark.

3. Before serving, add the pasta, if desired, and heat through. Adjust seasoning if necessary. Add 1 full table-spoon of the pistou to each serving of soup.

ONE SERVING: 369 Calories; 20.4 grams Fat (2.8 Saturated); 0 mg Cholesterol.

VARIATION: Experiment with other wines. Zinfandel, for example, has a fruity taste—often reminiscent of blackberries—that goes very well in gazpacho.

HINT: How to chop the vegetables is a matter of personal preference. Some like a bowl of tomatoes, celery, and cucumbers so finely minced that it is hard to recognize them; others demand a robust chop that leaves no doubt that the bounty of a summer's garden has been placed before them.

NOTE: Black beans are small, oval-shaped beans also known as turtle beans. An essential ingredient in many Hispanic recipes, they are dried and sold in Latin American specialty stores and most supermarkets.

VINO GAZPACHO

At the Tack Room in Tucson, Arizona, Chef David Lalli revives the classic salad-in-a-soupbowl with the addition of a dry chablis.

6 Servings
Preparation Time: 15 minutes
Chilling Time: 24 hours

1¾ lb. chopped fresh tomatoes
¾ cup chopped celery
¾ cup chopped green onion
¾ cup chopped cucumbers
2 cloves fresh garlic, minced
3 tbsp. red wine vinegar
1 tsp. Worcestershire sauce
1½ tbsp. Maggi seasoning
1½ cups beef stock
1 14-oz. can pitted black olives, sliced
¾ cup chablis wine
Tabasco sauce to taste
chopped chives
croutons (optional)

1. Combine all ingredients, except chives and croutons, and chill for 24 hours.

2. Garnish with chopped chives and croutons if desired, and serve.

ONE SERVING (Without garnish): 86 Calories; 0.6 grams Fat; 0 mg Cholesterol.

GLORIA'S BLACK BEAN SOUP

The name *Yuca* has double significance—as an acronym for Young Upscale Cuban Americans, and as a menu item in the restaurant of the same name. The restaurant Yuca, which serves yuca, a potato-like tuber, is creating a sensation in Miami. It was named as one of Conde Nast's Top Fifty Restaurants in America. Chef Douglas Rodriguez was nominated as one of the top four "rising star" chefs by the James Beard Foundation. This is a classic Cuban recipe from the mother of Yuca's chef, Douglas Rodriguez. The amount of oil used in sautéing the vegetables has been reduced, but the supercharged flavor remains the same.

8 Servings
Soaking Time: Overnight
Cooking Time: 4 hours

1 lb. dry black beans,
    washed and picked
    over
3 qt. water
2 bay leaves
2 tbsp. virgin olive oil
1 small onion (4 oz.),
    diced
1 large red bell pepper,
    coarsely chopped
1 large green bell pepper,
    coarsely chopped
3 small shallots, diced
2 tbsp. minced garlic
1 tbsp. ground cumin

1 tbsp. dried leaf oregano
2 tbsp. chopped fresh
    oregano
2 tbsp. chopped fresh
    parsley
1 tbsp. sugar
1 tbsp. salt

Garnish:

4 scallions, white and
    green, finely chopped
½ cup fat-reduced sour
    cream

1. In a large, heavy pot, soak the beans overnight in 3 quarts of water.

2. The next day, add bay leaves to beans and water and bring to a boil. Simmer, uncovered, over low heat for 3 to 4 hours, or until tender. (Beans will split open.) Stir occasionally and add water if necessary.

3. Heat a large, heavy-bottomed skillet over medium-high heat, then add olive oil. Add onion, red and green pepper, and shallots. Sauté until the onions are translucent. Add garlic, cumin, dried and fresh oregano, and parsley. Sauté for 30 seconds more. Add sugar and salt.

4. In a food processor or blender, throroughly purée onion-pepper mixture from skillet. Add purée to beans and cook for 20 to 30 minutes more. Correct seasoning. The soup will be very thick. Add water if a thinner soup is desired.

5. Garnish with chopped scallions and a dollop of sour cream.

ONE SERVING (Without topping): 204 Calories; 7.9 grams Fat (1.1 Saturated); 0 mg Cholesterol.

HEALTH TIP: Serving a meal based on the goodness of beans is what nutritionists recommend for a healthy approach to meal planning. Instead of centering the menu around meat, think of low-fat, high-protein beans. All varieties are rich in the fiber and complex carbohydrates that have been shown to be essential in reducing the risk of heart disease and cancer.

NOTE: Fresh lemongrass is available at some Asian markets. The citrus-scented blades add a distinctive flavor to Thai and Indonesian cooking. As a substitute for the fresh lemongrass in this recipe, you may use 1 teaspoon powdered or the yellow part of the peel from 1 lemon.

MAKE AHEAD: If you prefer, make this up to a day early and serve well chilled.

TROPICAL FRUIT SOUP

All nutritional guidelines suggest that we eat more fruit. How better can we comply than with this spectacular soup? Served as dessert at Le Bernardin in New York City, it is equally delightful as a first course.

6 Servings
Preparation Time: 30 minutes
Cooling Time: About 1 hour

1 clove
½ tsp. five-spice powder
1 vanilla bean, halved
    lengthwise
freshly grated zest of
    2 oranges
freshly grated zest of
    2 limes
1 tbsp. minced fresh
    ginger
2 tbsp. chopped fresh
    lemongrass
⅔ cup sugar
4½ cups water
1 mango, peeled, pitted,
    and thinly sliced

½ pineapple, peeled, core
    discarded, and the
    fruit thinly sliced
2 kiwis, peeled and thinly
    sliced
1 papaya, peeled, seeded,
    and thinly sliced
1 star fruit (carambola),
    thinly sliced
    (optional)
juice of 3 passion fruits
    (optional)
2 tbsp. thinly sliced fresh
    mint leaves
½ cup raspberries for
    garnish

1. In a medium saucepan, combine the clove, five-spice powder, vanilla bean, zests, ginger, lemongrass, sugar, and water. Bring to a boil, remove from heat and allow to cool completely. Strain through a fine sieve into a bowl.

2. To serve, divide mango, pineapple, kiwi, papaya, and star fruit slices among 6 bowls. Top the fruits with the syrup, passion-fruit juice (optional), mint, and raspberries.

ONE SERVING: 148 Calories; 0.3 grams Fat; 0 mg Cholesterol.

GOLDEN GAZPACHO
WITH BAY SCALLOPS

If we eat differently now than we used to, Chef Stephan Pyles is probably one of the reasons. His way of featuring fresh, Southwestern ingredients helped write the new book on American cuisine. His Routh Street Cafe was named the fifth best restaurant in America by London's *Courvosier's Book of the Best.* Cheers! Here is a bowl full of pleasure for your palate and a day's supply of vitamins for your vitality!

4 8-oz. servings
Preparation Time: 40 minutes
Chilling Time: At least one hour

8 oz. bay scallops
3 serrano chilies (stems
    and seeds removed),
    diced
¾ cup chicken stock
⅓ tsp. saffron
5 large golden tomatoes
    (about 4 cups),
    peeled, seeded, and
    diced
¼ cup yellow bell pepper,
    diced
⅓ cup cantaloupe, peeled
    and diced

⅓ cup papaya, peeled,
    seeded, and diced
⅓ cup mango, peeled,
    seeded, and diced
1 cucumber, peeled,
    seeded, and diced
¼ cup jicama, peeled and
    diced
6 scallions, white part
    only, diced
2 tbsp. lime juice
½ tsp. salt

1. Poach scallops. Drain and chill.

2. In a blender, purée the serrano chilies in the chicken stock. Add the saffron, then transfer to small bowl and let infuse for about 10 minutes.

3. In a large bowl, combine diced tomatoes, yellow peppers, cantaloupe, papaya, mango, cucumber, jicama, and scallions.

4. In processor or blender, purée ¾ of the tomato-fruit mixture; then add it back to ingredients in mixing bowl.

5. Strain chicken stock into the bowl and stir in lime juice and salt.

HEALTH TIP: Jicama (hee'-ka-ma) is a root vegetable indigenous to Mexico that resembles a large, brown turnip. Use it with abandon—jicama has almost no calories. It lends itself well to a variety of dishes—try it as a substitute for water chestnuts in salads and stir-fry dishes.

6. Let soup chill for at least one hour.

7. To serve, divide between 4 chilled soup bowls and top with 2 ounces of poached scallops.

ONE SERVING: 181 Calories; 3.3 grams Fat; 22 mg Cholesterol.

BUTTERNUT SQUASH SOUP

This soup is a tonic for autumn appetites from Chef Louis Jadot at the Topnotch Resort in Stowe, Vermont.

4 Servings
Preparation Time: 15 minutes
Cooking Time: 1 hour

2 lb. butternut squash, peeled, seeded, and chopped
1 tart green apple, peeled, cored, and chopped
1 cup chopped onion
3 cups chicken stock or canned low-salt broth

1 bay leaf
1 fresh rosemary sprig
2 fresh thyme sprigs
1 garlic clove
salt and pepper
sliced green onions for garnish

1. In a large, heavy saucepan, combine squash, apple, onion, and stock. Place bay leaf, rosemary, thyme, and garlic in a cheesecloth square; tie ends of packet securely with string and add to saucepan. Bring contents to a boil; then reduce heat, cover, and simmer until squash is very tender, about 30 minutes. Cool slightly and remove cheesecloth packet.

2. In a food processor or blender, purée soup until smooth. Season with salt and pepper. Ladle soup into bowls. Garnish with green onions and serve.

ONE SERVING: 119 Calories; 2.3 grams Fat; 0 mg Cholesterol.

MUSHROOM BARLEY SOUP

The recipe for this deliciously wholesome soup will probably become a treasured family heirloom, so don't forget to credit chef Alma Vactor! There are a lot of stars in the Southwestern sky, but The Tack Room in Tucson is the only one wearing 5 of them from Mobil. Chef Alma Vactor's reputation is based on her belief that great gourmet food should be just as healthy as it is delicious.

Makes 2½ quarts
Preparation Time: 30 minutes
Cooking Time: 2½ hours

1½ oz. dried mushrooms	2 large onions, chopped
1 large marrow or knuckle bone	½ tsp. garlic powder
	2 tsp. seasoned salt
2 lb. flank steak, in large pieces	1 28-oz. can tomatoes, drained and chopped (reserve liquid)
2 bay leaves	
1 tsp. pepper	1 qt. water
28 oz. beef broth	⅓ lb. barley
3 carrots, chopped	1 lb. fresh mushrooms, sliced
3 stalks celery, sliced	

1. Soak dried mushrooms in warm water until soft. Reserve liquid.

2. In a large soup pot, combine all ingredients except barley and mushrooms. Bring to boil, reduce heat, cover, and simmer for 1½ hours.

3. Remove and discard bones and bay leaves. Remove meat, shred, and return to pot. Add barley, fresh mushrooms, dried mushrooms, and mushroom soaking liquid. Adjust seasonings, adding more salt and pepper if desired. Add additional water if mixture is too thick. Simmer for 1 hour, or until barley is tender.

ONE SERVING (8 oz.): 281 Calories; 11.5 grams Fat (4.4 Saturated); 86 mg Cholesterol.

HEALTH TIP: The importance of grains in a healthy diet cannot be overstated. Barley, however, is one grain that has been largely overlooked—except by beer makers. Nutrition watchers should know that one cup of cooked barley contains six grams of protein; less than one gram of fat; practically no sodium; generous amounts of niacin, thiamin, and potassium; and only about 230 calories.

HINT: Curry powder looses its flavor as it sits in the jar. If yours has been on the shelf for longer than a few months, let your nose decide if the pungency has gone. The success of this dish depends on the seasoning power of a first-rate curry.

NOTE: Cooks on tropical islands—even great chefs—have difficulty getting fresh carrots and peas because these vegetables do not grow well in hot climates. If you prefer, substitute garden vegetables for the frozen variety in this recipe. The cooking time is almost the same.

CARIBBEAN CURRIED SOUP

In out-of-the-way little Statia, which truly is the Caribbean the way you would like it to be, The Old Gin House serves guests on the terrace under the stars. This soup exemplifies the simple tropical taste of The Old Gin House Resort, St. Eustatius, Netherlands Antilles.

6 Servings
Preparation Time: 30 minutes

2 tbsp. calorie-reduced margarine	1 10-oz. pkg. frozen peas
1 medium onion, diced	1 tbsp. curry powder
5 cups chicken broth	salt and pepper to taste
1 medium potato, peeled and diced	¼ lb. seedless green grapes
1 10-oz. pkg. frozen carrots	chopped parsley for garnish

1. In a large saucepan, heat 1 tablespoon of the margarine. Add onion and cook until golden. Add broth, potatoes, and carrots. Bring to a boil, reduce heat, then cook until vegetables are tender, about 10 minutes.

2. Add peas and curry powder. Taste for seasoning. Add salt and pepper to taste. Cook for 1 minute.

3. In a blender or food processor, blend in small batches, until smooth. Return to heat and bring to a simmer. Stir in the remaining 1 tablespoon of margarine, then remove from heat.

4. To serve, cut grapes in halves, divide between soup bowls, and pour hot soup over grapes. Garnish with chopped parsley.

ONE SERVING: 155 Calories; 2.7 grams Fat; 10 mg Cholesterol.

THE RUSSIAN TEA ROOM BORSCHT

Served with a chunk of dark bread, this soup from the world-famous restaurant in New York City provides nourishment for the soul on a winter's day.

8 Servings
Preparation Time: 15 minutes (does not include stock preparation)
Cooking Time: 50 minutes

Stock:

1 beef soup bone (about 1 lb.)
1 cup chopped onion
1 cup chopped celery
½ cup chopped parsley
2 tomatoes, peeled and chopped
1 small cabbage, cored, outer leaves removed, and chopped
1 tsp. salt (optional)
8 cups water

Borscht:

1 cup chopped onion
½ cup grated carrots
3 cups finely shredded cabbage
1 29-oz. can tomato sauce
1 20-oz. can whole beets, drained and julienned (reserve liquid)
2 tbsp. lemon juice
salt and freshly ground pepper
cayenne pepper (optional)
fat-reduced sour cream or nonfat yogurt (optional)

MAKE AHEAD: A slow cooker can be a help with this recipe. Simmer the stock ingredients overnight, then the time in the kitchen the next day will be reduced to about an hour.

1. Combine all stock ingredients, bring to a boil, reduce heat and simmer for at least three hours. Strain.

2. In a large soup pot, heat 8 cups of the stock. Add onion, carrots, cabbage, and tomato sauce. Bring to a boil, then reduce heat and simmer for 30 minutes, stirring occasionally.

3. Add beets and all of the liquid from the can of beets. Continue to cook for about 10 minutes. Taste for seasoning. Add lemon juice, salt, and peppers to taste.

4. Remove from heat. Top with low-fat sour cream or yogurt, if desired.

ONE SERVING (One Cup): 89 Calories; 3.6 grams Fat; 0 Cholesterol.

Salads

Salads

Turkey Paillard with Cucumber Thai Salad
Grilled Marinated Vegetable Cobb Salad
Brown and Wild Rice Salad
Arugula and Fried Okra Salad with Roast Corn Vinaigrette
Stove Top Pasta Salad
Belgian Endive and Orange Salad
Asparagus Salad with Herb Dressing
Opryland Garlic Dressing
Salmon Salad with Cilantro Mayonnaise
Rock Shrimp and Roast Corn Salad
Marinated Halibut Salad
Blackened Jumbo Scallops with Ferns and Watercress Salad
Garden Salad with Smoked Tomato Dressing
Pong Pong Chicken Salad
Jody's Fire and Ice Tomatoes
Vegetable Salad with Truffle Dressing
Crunchy Lunch
Romaine with Beet and Garlic Dressing

HINT: Fish sauce, made
from salted fresh shrimp
or fish, is an indispens-
able flavoring in South-
east Asian cooking.
Milder in flavor than soy
sauce, it is used to im-
part a salty flavor to Thai
dishes. It can be found in
any Asian market and
some grocery stores.

*HINT: Fish sauce, made
from salted fresh shrimp
or fish, is an indispens-
able flavoring in South-
east Asian cooking.
Milder in flavor than soy
sauce, it is used to im-
part a salty flavor to Thai
dishes. It can be found in
any Asian market and
some grocery stores.*

*HEALTH TIP: Perfect for
today's healthy recipes, a
paillard is a thin piece of
chicken, beef, or veal that
is well-seasoned and
cooked very rapidly with-
out fat.*

TURKEY PAILLARD
WITH CUCUMBER THAI SALAD

Chef Jean-Marie Lacroix seasons this salad with a Thai
vinaigrette, then makes it more substantial by adding peppery rounds of quickly grilled turkey. In Philadelphia, the elegant Four Seasons restaurant features "Alternate
Cuisine"—daily menu items that are low in sodium, fat,
cholesterol, and calories.

4 Servings
Preparation and Cooking Time: 20 minutes

**4 3-oz. turkey cutlets,
    pounded thin
freshly ground pepper
⅓ cup fresh lime juice
½ cup olive oil
¼ cup Thai fish sauce
¼ red chili paste**

**2 large cucumbers,
    peeled, seeded, and
    julienned
20 cherry tomatoes, cut
    in half
4 tsp. chopped fresh
    cilantro
4 tsp. chopped fresh mint**

1. Preheat grill.

2. To prepare paillards, season pounded turkey cutlet with
pepper. Grill (or sauté in a hot, non-stick skillet) for 1 or 2
minutes on each side.

3. In a small bowl, whisk together the lime juice, olive oil,
fish sauce, and chili paste to make the Thai vinaigrette. Do
not add salt.

4. Combine cucumbers, tomatoes, cilantro, and mint. Toss
with Thai vinaigrette.

5. To serve, divide the cucumber and tomato salad onto four
plates and top each with a turkey paillard.

ONE SERVING: 410 Calories; 31 grams Fat (4.7 Saturated);
58 mg Cholesterol.

GRILLED MARINATED VEGETABLE COBB SALAD

The traditional Cobb salad, which originated in California, included high-fat bacon and blue cheese. This up-to-date version is much lighter, and it's one of the prettiest salads you'll ever serve! It's just one of Chef Steven Petusevsky's creations at Miami's upscale natural food restaurant, Unicorn Village. Every dish is prepared from scratch and features the freshest, healthiest ingredients available. The menu even offers a list of organic wines and beers.

4 Servings
Preparation Time: 40 minutes

½ cup olive oil
¼ cup lemon juice
2 cloves garlic, minced
salt to taste
1 10-oz. pkg. silken tofu
¼ cup tamari sauce (or
    low-sodium soy
    sauce)
1½ lb. mixed greens
    (romaine, escarole,
    spinach, leaf lettuce)
4½-inch slices eggplant,
    cut lengthwise
1 large red onion, peeled
    and sliced ½ inch
    thick

4½-inch lengthwise
    slices yellow squash
1 red bell pepper, halved
    and seeded
1 green bell pepper,
    halved and seeded
1 ripe avocado, peeled
    and diced
1 ripe tomato, diced
8 oz. soy cheese (or fat-
    reduced Monterey
    Jack), crumbled

1. Preheat grill and turn oven to broil.

2. Combine olive oil, lemon juice, garlic, and salt and blend well to make a marinade for the vegetables.

3. Sprinkle tofu with tamari sauce. Place under broiler and broil on both sides until light golden brown. Dice into bite-sized pieces and set aside.

4. Brush eggplant, onion, squash, and bell peppers with vegetable marinade. Grill until tender, but still crisp. Cut eggplant, squash, and peppers into 1-inch cubes.

VARIATION: Salads may be presented untossed as directed, or may be mixed with a simple vinaigrette dressing before serving.

HEALTH TIP: High-protein tofu, the delicately flavored white soybean custard, contains only 20 calories per ounce. Sometimes referred to as the "cheese of the Asians," it absorbs other flavors readily.

5. Divide salad greens onto 4 chilled plates. Arrange colorful bands of eggplant, squash, peppers, tomatoes, avocado, diced tofu, and soy cheese on greens. Garnish with grilled onion slices.

ONE SERVING: 279 Calories; 20.6 grams Fat (9.8 Saturated); 50 mg Cholesterol.

BROWN AND WILD RICE SALAD

This is a lusty, bountiful salad from Chef Paula Sideras, a vegetarian whose cooking school classes have introduced scores of students in Dayton, Ohio, to the delicious benefits of grains and vegetables. For those with more good intentions than time, Sideras' catering business features a variety of healthy gourmet-to-go dishes.

6 Servings
Preparation Time: 1½ hours

2 cups brown rice
½ cup wild rice
5 cups water
1 cup pecan pieces
1 cup sun dried tomatoes (not in oil), slivered
¼ cup oil-cured olives, pitted and quartered

4 green onions, sliced thin
½ cup parsley, minced
8 large basil leaves, thinly sliced
¼ cup olive oil
salt and pepper
roasted red peppers (optional)

1. In a medium heavy pot, combine brown rice, wild rice, and water. Cover and bring to a boil; then lower heat and simmer for 50 minutes. Transfer immediately to a large, shallow dish to cool.

2. When nearly cool, transfer the rice to a large bowl and combine it with the remaining ingredients. Season with salt and pepper to taste. Garnish with roasted red peppers if desired. Serve at room temperature.

ONE SERVING: 315.5 Calories; 22.4 grams Fat (2.4 Saturated); 0 mg Cholesterol.

IN A HURRY? Roasted red peppers can be purchased, ready to use, in jars at most grocery stores.

HEALTH TIP: Be in the one percent crowd—it is estimated that one percent of the people in this country choose brown rice over white. Once you discover the delicious, nutty flavor and realize its benefits over the denuded white variety, it may become your first choice.

ARUGULA AND FRIED OKRA SALAD WITH ROAST CORN VINAIGRETTE

This robust salad with a southern accent comes from Routh Street Cafe in Dallas. The chef, Stephan Pyles, was one of the first to be honored with the coveted title of "Great American Chef" by the James Beard Foundation. The criteria for selection are making a significant contribution to fine cooking in America and gaining a national reputation as a great chef.

6 Servings
Preparation Time: 45 minutes

1 cup corn kernels (cut from about 5 roasted ears)
1 tbsp. minced shallots
1 tsp. minced garlic
⅓ cup chicken stock
1 tbsp. white wine vinegar
½ cup corn oil
⅓ cup olive oil
salt to taste
1 egg

2 tbsp. milk
salted cornmeal
cooking oil
10 large okra spears (tips and stems removed), sliced into ¼-inch rounds
6 cups arugula
1 medium tomato, blanched, peeled, seeded, and diced

1. Prepare grill or preheat oven to 400 degrees.

2. In a blender or food processor, purée the corn, shallots, and garlic with the chicken stock and vinegar. Combine the corn oil with the olive oil. With the motor running on low speed, slowly drizzle the oils into the corn mixture. Season to taste with salt. Set aside.

3. In a shallow bowl, combine egg and milk. Dip okra rounds into egg wash, then dredge in cornmeal. In a small skillet, heat ¼ inch of oil. When the oil is lightly smoking, cook okra for about 2 minutes, stirring occasionally. Remove, drain well, and keep warm.

4. Place arugula in a mixing bowl and drizzle with the vinaigrette. Toss thoroughly and divide among 6 plates. Top with okra and tomato.

HINT: To roast corn, grill on a rack 5 to 6 inches over hot coals or in a preheated 400-degree oven for about 15 minutes, turning occasionally with tongs. Cut kernels from ears with a sharp knife.

NOTE: Arugula, sometimes known as roquette or garden rocket, is not so prominent in American produce markets, but is known and loved by all European salad makers. It has a peppery taste that mixes well with milder greens. If arugula is not available for this salad, try using a mix of curly endive and shredded leaf lettuce.

ONE SERVING: 299 Calories; 27.6 grams Fat (4.8 Saturated); 0 mg Cholesterol.

STOVE TOP PASTA SALAD

At Chicago's Ritz-Carlton, Chef Pascal Vignau cooks the vegetables for this snappy salad on the flat, hot surface of his professional range top. You will probably choose to use a skillet, but the results are still delightful!

4 Servings
Preparation Time: 35 minutes

3 tbsp. olive oil
3 leeks (white part only), chopped
1 cup young, tender green beans, in 1-inch pieces
½ cup red bell pepper, julienned
½ cup yellow bell pepper, julienned
½ cup shitake mushrooms, stems removed, julienned

4 large garlic cloves, minced
4 anchovies, minced
2 cups pasta, cooked al dente and drained
1 red tomato, chopped
3 tbsp. balsamic vinegar
salt and pepper
2 cups medium-sized spinach leaves
2 scallions, slivered

1. In a large, heavy skillet, heat 1 tablespoon olive oil; then add leeks and stir-fry for 1 minute. Add beans and stir-fry for 1 minute; then add peppers and stir-fry for 1 minute. Add mushrooms, garlic, and anchovies and stir-fry for 1 last minute.

2. In a large bowl, toss vegetable mixture with pasta, tomato, vinegar, and remaining 2 tablespoons olive oil. Taste for seasoning and add a little salt and freshly ground pepper if desired. Serve on a bed of spinach leaves and top with scallions.

ONE SERVING: 273 Calories; 15.1 grams Fat (2.1 Saturated); 0 mg Cholesterol.

HINT: The size and shape of rotelle pasta makes it a good match for the julienned vegetables.

BELGIAN ENDIVE
AND ORANGE SALAD

A most elegant vegetable combines with sherry and fruit to makes a spirited salad that will add only 72 calories and 1 gram of fat to your day's total. When *Bon Appetit* magazine selected the "Finest Meal in St. Louis," honors went to Fio's La Fourchette. Chef Fio Antognini features an entire meal with less than 750 calories, proving that he can offer diners a satisfying feast for the senses—even for the sense of self-discipline!

4 Servings
Preparation Time: 30 minutes

4 Belgian endives	½ tsp. chopped garlic
6 tbsp. plain low-fat yogurt	2 tsp. dry sherry
1 tsp. curry powder	2 oranges, peeled and sectioned
2 tsp. orange juice	chopped parsley
2 tsp. lemon juice	

1. Trim and soak endives in water for 15 to 20 minutes. Separate leaves.

2. In a small bowl, whisk together the yogurt, curry powder, orange juice, lemon juice, garlic, and sherry.

3. On each of 4 plates, arrange endives and orange sections; then pour yogurt dressing over all. Garnish with chopped parsley.

ONE SERVING: 72 Calories; 1.1 grams Fat; 3 mg Cholesterol.

TIP: Belgian endive weighs in at only about 18 calories per head. Look for compact heads with white, yellow-edged leaves. It has a slightly bitter taste that complements the curry in this salad.

ASPARAGUS SALAD
WITH HERB DRESSING

This artful salad comes from L'Auberge, the elegant restaurant in Dayton, Ohio where Chef Dieter Krug annually accepts Mobil's Four Stars, among other well-deserved awards.

NICE WITH: Asparagus is not known as an affectionate mate to wine, but a happy exception is Riesling. A chilled bottle from Alsace or one of the new California Rieslings would be lovely with this salad.

4 Servings
Preparation Time: 25 minutes

**24 stalks tender fresh
  asparagus**
bibb lettuce
1 tbsp. Dijon mustard
1 shallot, minced
¾ cup salad oil

salt and white pepper
2 tbsp. red wine vinegar
½ tbsp. lemon juice
**2 tbsp. minced fresh
  herbs**

1. Wash the asparagus, peel the stems off, and wash again. Place the asparagus in boiling, salted water just until tender, about 3 to 4 minutes. Plunge immediately in ice water to stop the cooking.

2. In a bowl, whisk together the mustard and shallots. Slowly add the oil in a steady steam. After the oil has been incorporated, whisk in the vinegar, lemon juice, and herbs.

3. Place the drained asparagus on a bed of lettuce and top with dressing.

ONE SERVING: 186 Calories; 18.9 grams Fat (2.6 Saturated); 0 mg Cholesterol.

OPRYLAND GARLIC DRESSING

In Nashville, diners at the Opryland Restaurant sit in a tropical conservatory and listen to the music of country and western's greats. This lightened version of their creamy house salad dressing could make you feel like singing!

Makes 1 cup
Preparation Time: 10 minutes

**¾ cup low-calorie
  mayonnaise**
¼ cup white wine vinegar
**½ cup finely chopped
  celery**

**½ cup finely chopped
  onion**
4 cloves garlic, minced
½ tsp. anchovy paste
⅛ tsp. oregano
⅛ tsp. white pepper

1. Combine all ingredients in a food processor or blender and blend thoroughly. Refrigerate and use within one week. Serve with your choice of crisp salad ingredients.

ONE SERVING (1 tablespoon): 55 Calories; 3.5 grams Fat; 6 mg Cholesterol.

SALMON SALAD
WITH CILANTRO MAYONNAISE

Joining the fruits of land and sea, the ingredients in this salad create a profusion of both color and taste. The recipe was adapted from one created by Chef Stephan Pyles. The Routh Street Cafe in Dallas, Texas is one of only a handful of restaurants named to the Fine Dining Hall of Fame.

4-6 Servings
Preparation Time: 25 minutes

1 cup (8 oz.) cooked
    salmon, lightly flaked
1 tbsp. diced red bell
    pepper
1 tbsp. diced yellow bell
    pepper
1 tbsp. diced carrot
2 tbsp. diced jicama
3 tbsp. diced papaya
2 tbsp. diced red seedless
    grapes
3 tbsp. thawed frozen
    English peas

3 tbsp. roasted pine nuts
⅓ cup low-fat
    mayonnaise
2 tbsp. chopped cilantro
1 tbsp. chopped shallot
1 tsp. chopped chives or
    green onion tops
1 tsp. chopped parsley
1 tsp. lemon juice
salt and freshly ground
    pepper to taste

HEALTH TIP: Salmon is high in protein as well as a rich source of vitamins A and B as well as Omega-3 oils. Pink salmon, the delicate variety from the Pacific ocean, is lower in fat than sockeye salmon or king salmon.

MAKE AHEAD: This salad can be prepared up to twenty-four hours in advance. Refrigerate until about an hour before serving.

VARIATION: Fresh cooked tuna or other firm fish can be substituted for the salmon. When planning to serve grilled fish, purchase one half pound extra to be cooked, chilled, and flaked, ready for the next day's delicious salad.

1. In a large mixing bowl, combine the first nine ingredients.

2. In a small bowl, whisk together remaining ingredients to make cilantro mayonnaise.

3. Lightly toss salad and cilantro mayonnaise together and serve.

ONE SERVING: 257 Calories; 11.0 grams Fat (1.7 Saturated); 39 mg Cholesterol.

IN A HURRY?: One cup of defrosted frozen corn may be substituted for the roasted corn.

ROCK SHRIMP AND ROAST CORN SALAD

Chef Mark Meyer combines shrimp and peppers with the kick of an allspice-enhanced sauce. You can make this unusual salad up to two days before your guests arrive. Marc Meyer is chef at The Brasserie Savoy, a recipient of the Conde Nast Distinguished Restaurant Award. *Gourmet* magazine calls it "one of the best new restaurants in San Francisco."

4 to 6 Servings
Preparation Time: 2 hours

4 cups water
1 cup rice wine vinegar
1 cup apple cider vinegar
3 tbsp. sugar
2 tsp. salt
1 tbsp. cloves
1 tbsp. coriander seed
1 tbsp. mustard seed
1 cinnamon stick
1 dried chili pepper

4 cups rock shrimp
2 tbsp. olive oil
2 cups finely diced red bell pepper
2 cups finely diced green bell pepper
1 small red onion, finely diced
4 ears corn, roasted in the husk

1. To prepare the pickling liquid, combine the water, vinegars, sugar, salt, cloves, coriander, mustard, cinnamon, and chili pepper in a large non-corrosive pan. Bring to a boil and allow to simmer gently for 20 minutes; then turn off heat and cover pan. Allow mixture to steep for 45 minutes; then strain to remove spices and reserve the liquid. Allow to cool.

2. In a hot skillet, sear the shrimp just until they turn pink. Remove from the skillet and add olive oil. When the oil is hot, add peppers and onions and sauté until slightly tender.

3. Strip the roasted corn from the cob and add it and the shrimp to the skillet. Pour the cooled pickling liquid over the mixture. Mix together gently. Allow to sit for about 15 minutes before serving.

ONE SERVING: 129 Calories; 5.0 grams Fat; 95 mg Cholesterol.

MARINATED HALIBUT SALAD

Chef Fio Antognini makes this salad a main dish by combining grilled fish with a silken blend of yogurt, curry, and a dash of sherry. Mr. Antognini is proud of his focus on healthy eating at Fio's in St. Louis, Missouri. He features a special menu with a seasonal choice of low-fat, low-calorie selections.

HEALTH TIP: One serving of this salad provides almost twenty-five grams of protein. On a daily basis, forty-five grams of protein for women and fifty-five grams for men is generally thought to be adequate.

4 Servings
Preparation Time: 20 minutes
Marinate: At least 3 hours

8 oz. nonfat yogurt
¼ cup orange juice
2 tbsp. lemon juice
2 tbsp. soy sauce
1 tbsp. sherry
1 tbsp. curry powder
salt to taste
1 lb. halibut

freshly ground pepper
assorted greens (bib, radicchio, frisée, leaf lettuce, baby romaine, Belgian endive)
lemon wedges

1. In a small bowl, combine yogurt, orange juice, 1 tablespoon lemon juice, 1 tablespoon soy sauce, sherry curry powder, and salt. Mix thoroughly. Refrigerate for at least 3 hours, preferably overnight.

2. Trim halibut of all skin, bones, and dark meat. Cut halibut into small strips and cover with ground pepper, 1 tablespoon soy sauce and 1 tablespoon lemon juice. Marinate, refrigerated, for at least 3 hours.

3. When ready to serve, preheat oven to 375 degrees. Lay halibut strips on baking sheet and place in oven for 4 to 6 minutes, or until lightly firm.

4. Toss greens with ⅔ of the dressing. Place on serving plate, top with halibut, and drizzle remainder of dressing over all. Garnish with lemon wedges.

ONE SERVING: 153 Calories; 4.2 grams Fat; 60 mg Cholesterol.

HINT: *Cajun spice mix-tures can be found in the spice section of most food stores. Different brands vary in the amount of hot peppers included, so use them sparingly until you have determined the "fire-per-tablespoon" ratio.*

BLACKENED JUMBO SCALLOPS WITH FERNS AND WATERCRESS SALAD

If your garden bears no fresh ferns for the kitchen, you can still enjoy this refreshing salad. It's one of Chef George Mavrothalassitis' favorites at Orchids, the seaside restaurant at Halekulani Hotel in Honolulu. The hotel has been named one of the top ten United States hotels, and their French restaurant, La Mer, was selected by the International Institute for Dining Excellence to receive the prestigious Ambassador Award.

4 Servings
Preparation Time: 25 minutes

24 jumbo scallops
Cajun spices
1 tsp. unsalted butter
1 tbsp. garlic, chopped
½ cup French olive oil
¼ cup lemon juice
salt and pepper to taste

4 cups watercress leaves
2 cups baby fiddlehead ferns, blanched (or other greens)
4 tbsp. julienned red bell pepper

1. Season one side of each scallop with the Cajun spices. Preheat a cast iron skillet for 10 minutes. Add scallops, seasoned side down, and cook until blackened, about 2 minutes. Add butter, turn scallops, and cook on the other side for 1 minute. Remove scallops and set aside.

2. Whisk together the garlic, olive oil, and lemon juice with salt and pepper. Toss with the watercress, ferns (or other greens), and red pepper.

3. In the middle of four plates, arrange the tossed salad. Surround the greens with the scallops and serve immediately.

ONE SERVING: 240 Calories; 17.4 grams Fat (2.5 Saturated); 33 mg Cholesterol.

GARDEN SALAD
WITH SMOKED TOMATO
DRESSING

Remember how satisfying it was to bite into a BLT sandwich? Wait until you try this bacon, lettuce, and tomato salad with a new wave vinaigrette from Routh Street Cafe!

4 Servings
Preparation Time: 30 minutes

2 strips lean bacon, diced
1 large, ripe tomato
2 tsp. tomato paste
1 clove garlic, minced
1 shallot, peeled and
    diced
1 tsp. balsamic vinegar
2 tsp. raspberry vinegar

¼ cup corn oil
¼ cup olive oil
salt to taste
4 cups assorted young
    lettuce (romaine,
    bibb, arugula, oak
    leaf)

1. Preheat smoker.

2. Cook bacon, drain well, and pat with paper towels. Set aside.

3. Smoke tomato for 15 minutes. Remove from smoker and peel. Slice in half and squeeze liquid from tomato into a small saucepan. Add tomato paste and cook over medium heat for 2 minutes, stirring often.

4. Place tomato mixture, garlic, shallot, and vinegars in a blender. Purée for 30 seconds. With blender on low speed, slowly add the oils. Season with salt.

5. Place assorted lettuce in a large bowl. Toss gently with dressing. Divide among serving plates and top each salad with some of the reserved bacon.

ONE SERVING: 149 Calories; 16.0 grams Fat (2.6 Saturated); 3 mg Cholesterol.

HEALTH TIP: *Thinking of accompanying this salad with some bread? Reach for a chewy, dense, whole-grain bread for a more filling, satisfying, and nutrient-packed experience. Label detectives should look for the word "whole" in the first three ingredients. Try rye, pumpernickel, or cracked wheat for variety.*

PONG PONG CHICKEN SALAD

There are just 240 calories in this marvelous toss of vegetables, spice, and tender chicken from Chef Lucy Chu. Lucy Chu, the daughter-in-law of cookbook author Grace Chu, conducts cooking classes aboard the cruise ship *Queen Elizabeth II.*

4 Servings
Preparation Time: 25 minutes
Chill: At least 2 hours

2 cups fresh bean sprouts
½ cup shredded carrots
2 tbsp. peanut butter
2 tbsp. warm water
1 tbsp. sugar
½ tsp. salt
2 tbsp. soy sauce

1 tbsp. vinegar
1 tsp. Tabasco sauce
1 clove garlic, minced
2 tbsp. minced scallion
2 tbsp. vegetable oil
2 cups cooked chicken
  breast, shredded

1. Parboil the sprouts and the carrots separately for 10 seconds each. Rinse with cold water, drain, and set aside.

2. In a small bowl, mix together the peanut butter and water to make a thin, smooth paste. Add sugar, salt, soy sauce, vinegar, and Tabasco sauce.

3. Place garlic and scallions in another small bowl. Heat vegetable oil until very hot and pour over garlic and scallions. Add this mixture to the peanut sauce.

4. Toss shredded chicken, sprouts, and carrots with the peanut sauce. Refrigerate for at least 2 hours and serve chilled.

ONE SERVING: 240 Calories; 13.2 grams Fat (2.4 Saturated); 47 mg Cholesterol.

HEALTH TIP: Health-smart cooks look to the recipe treasures of China for a cuisine based on vegetables, grains, and only a small amount of meat.

NOTE: To parboil the bean sprouts, place in a colander, lower into boiling water and cook for one minute. This removes the strong taste, but leaves the sprouts tender and crunchy. Use the same method to parboil the shredded carrots, cooking for one to two minutes.

JODY'S FIRE AND ICE TOMATOES

At Le Dome in Fort Lauderdale, this salad is made with glorious summer beefsteak tomatoes and a slenderizing no-oil dressing. Le Dome was selected as "Number One Continental Restaurant" by the readers of *Fort Lauderdale Magazine*.

6 Servings
Preparation Time: 10 minutes
Chilling Time: At least 30 minutes

¾ cup vinegar
¼ cup water
1½ tsp. celery salt
4½ tsp. sugar
⅛ tsp. ground red pepper
   (not cayenne)

⅛ tsp. black pepper
2 large tomatoes, cut in
   ¼ to ½ inch slices
1 green pepper, sliced
   thin
1 red onion, sliced thin

1. In a small saucepan, combine vinegar, water, celery salt, sugar, red pepper, and black pepper. Bring to a boil and cook for one minute.

2. Layer sliced vegetables in a glass dish. Pour hot liquid over vegetables.

3. Chill and serve.

ONE SERVING: 42 Calories; 0.3 grams Fat ; 0 mg Cholesterol.

VEGETABLE SALAD
WITH TRUFFLE DRESSING

Dieting? Who could feel deprived with truffles on their plate? The Fountain at the Four Seasons Hotel in Philadelphia features eclectic cuisine, which Chef Jean-Marie Lacroix says is "imaginative and unfussy" in the use of fresh ingredients, including locally grown organic produce.

4 Servings
Preparation Time: 20 minutes
Marinate: 25 minutes

HEALTH TIP: The unprejudiced palate learns to savor salads tossed with dressings based on vinegar instead of oil. It is quite common in Germany, for example, to be served a first course salad of freshly cut vegetables adorned with just a splash of flavored vinegar.

HEALTH TIP: Are mushrooms low in calories? One ounce of truffle, the noblest mushroom, has a mere twenty-eight calories.

½ cup snow peas, strings removed and freshened in cold water
½ cup cauliflower, cut into florets
½ cup julienned red bell pepper
½ cup julienned yellow squash
½ cup julienned tomato
1 dried black truffle, soaked
2 tbsp. truffle soaking liquid
4 tbsp. virgin olive oil
salt and pepper

1. In a large saucepan of boiling water, blanch peas, cauliflower, pepper, and squash. Immediately plunge into cold water and drain; then combine with tomato in a bowl.

2. Blend together the remaining ingredients, pour over vegetables, and marinate for 30 minutes. Serve garnished with slivers of black truffle.

ONE SERVING: 166 Calories; 14.2 grams Fat (1.9 Saturated); 0 mg Cholesterol.

CRUNCHY LUNCH

Chef Marian Stapleton, a consultant to health spas, says, "This salad is packed with nourishment and chewing power, and the savory vinaigrette will become a staple in your refrigerator!"

4 Servings
Preparation Time: 10 minutes

3 cloves garlic, peeled
¾ cup red wine vinegar
2 tbsp. fresh lemon juice
1 tbsp. Dijon mustard
1 individual pkg. sugar substitute
dash pepper
2 tsp. dried oregano
2 tbsp. chopped parsley
¼ cup olive oil
4 small bunches watercress, stems removed
1 cup chopped radishes
1 cup thinly sliced celery
2 cup chopped alfalfa sprouts
½ cup grated low-fat mozzarella

HEALTH TIP: No salt is needed in this tasty salad. Remember that one teaspoon of salt has 1,200 milligrams of sodium. All that is recommended for the day's total sodium intake is one to three thousand milligrams.

1. In food processor, combine first eight ingredients and blend well. Slowly add the olive oil. Chill.

2. Toss remaining ingredients together well. Toss with ½ cup of the vinaigrette. Serve on four chilled serving plates. Store the remaining dressing in the refrigerator.

ONE SERVING: 170 Calories; 3.9 grams Fat; 21 mg Cholesterol.

ROMAINE WITH BEET
AND GARLIC DRESSING

This recipe is a delicious example of the contemporary "Great Lakes Cuisine" served by Chef Patrick Dunn at Van Dyke Place in Detroit, Michigan.

4 Servings
Preparation Time: 1 hour

1 lb. fresh young beets
3 large garlic cloves,
   minced
½ cup balsamic vinegar
1½ cup extra virgin olive
   oil

dash Worcestershire
   sauce
salt and pepper
1 head romaine lettuce,
   washed, dried, and
   chopped (about
   4 cups)

1. Cook beets in boiling water until tender, about 40 minutes for small, young beets. Drain and allow to cool slightly.

2. In a food processor or blender, purée beets, garlic, and vinegar until smooth. Slowly add the oil until completely emulsified. Season with Worcestershire sauce, salt, and pepper.

3. For four servings, toss the greens with about ½ cup of the dressing. Store the remaining dressing in the refrigerator.

ONE SERVING: 143 Calories; 14.1 grams Fat (1.9 Saturated); 0 mg Cholesterol.

HINT: For this salad, find the youngest beets imaginable. Barely nubile beets plucked from a garden are a completely different vegetable from the old and tired ones found lingering on some produce shelves.

Pasta

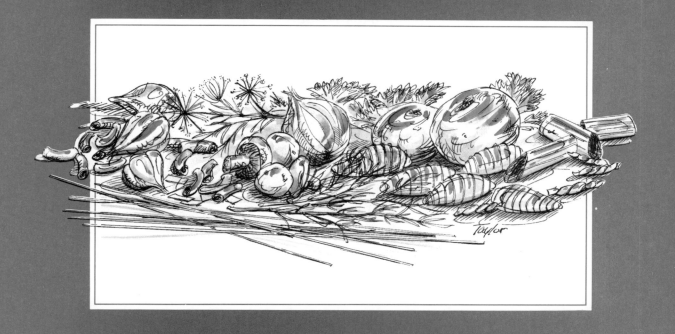

Pasta

Pasta Primavera

Key Lime Linguine with Crab and Pommery Mustard Sauce

Italian Red Pepper Pesto

Angel Hair Pasta with Chicken, Basil, and Olives

Rigatoni with Apples and Bacon in a Peppered Vodka Sauce

Pasta with Sundried and Fresh Tomato Sauce

Pasta with Smoked Salmon and Dill

Pasta with Goat Cheese, Tomato, and Cucumber

Bangkok Pasta

Ziti Italiano

Cappellini with Grilled Swordfish, Baby Vegetables,
and Herb Broth

Artichoke Ravioli with Tomato Compote

Udon Noodle, Shitake Mushroom, and Green Onion
Pancakes with Peanut-Miso Sauce

Tortelloni Kahala

PASTA PRIMAVERA

HINT: Capelli D'Angelo, the thinnest of all pasta, cooks in one or two minutes. Capellini, which is only slightly thicker and may be easier to find, cooks in three or four minutes.

TIP: If you have access to a resourceful cheese merchant, ask for Parmigiano-Reggiano. This is the Ferrari of cheeses from the Parma region of Italy. It is expensive, but this dish is worth it.

Chef Mario Gattorna at Il Gattopardo in New York City says, "This is what we recommend for diners who request something light. It is the very best recipe for Angel Hair Pasta Primavera!"

4 Servings
Preparation Time: 1 hour

½ cup finely chopped lean prosciutto
¼ cup finely chopped lean pancetta (Italian bacon)
½ cup chopped onion
½ cup sliced fresh mushrooms
1 cup chicken broth
½ cup white wine

½ cup green beans, cut into ½-inch pieces
½ cup zucchini, cut into thin ½-inch strips
½ cup frozen green peas
1 finely diced tomato
salt and freshly ground pepper
1 lb. angel hair pasta
freshly grated parmesan cheese

1. Heat water for pasta.

2. In a large, non-stick skillet, sauté the prosciutto and pancetta for 5 minutes. Add onion and mushrooms, then cook for 5 more minutes.

3. Meanwhile, in a large saucepan, bring the broth and wine to a boil. Add the beans, cook for 3 minutes, then add the zucchini and peas. Cook on medium-high until vegetables are crisp and tender, about 5 minutes.

4. Combine bacon-onion mixture with the vegetables. Add tomato and season to taste with salt and pepper.

5. Cook pasta in boiling water for 1 to 2 minutes. Drain.

6. To serve, arrange drained pasta on plate. Top with sauce and parmesan cheese.

ONE SERVING: 311 Calories; 10.1 grams Fat (3.5 Saturated); 15 mg Cholesterol.

KEY LIME LINGUINE
WITH CRAB AND POMMERY
MUSTARD SAUCE

Chef Allen Susser, one of *Food and Wine* magazine's "America's Best New Chefs," creates pasta magic at Chef Allen's in Miami, Florida. Chef Susser features New World cuisine with influences from the Caribbean, Latin America, and modern America, using mostly local products. Bryan Miller of the *New York Times* wrote, "It could be argued that Allen Susser is the Ponce de Leon of new Florida cooking."

4 Servings
Preparation Time: 20 minutes
Cooking Time: 10 minutes

1 lb. stone crab
1 tbsp. olive oil
2 medium shallots, minced
2 tbsp. Dijon mustard
1/4 cup Pommery mustard
1/2 cup white wine
1 cup half-and-half
1/4 tsp. cayenne pepper
4 qt. water
1 tbsp. salt
1 lb. fresh key lime pasta (or fresh linguine plus 1 tbsp. lime juice)

1. Crack the crab well and remove all the meat from the knuckles and claws. Set aside.

2. In a large sauté pan, heat the olive oil and add the shallots. Cook slowly for one minute; then add the two mustards and white wine. Cook, stirring, for one minute; then add the crab, half-and-half, and cayenne pepper.

3. In a large pot, boil four quarts of water with 1 tablespoon of salt. Cook the fresh pasta al dente for about 2 to 4 minutes. Drain. (If using linguine, pour lime juice over drained pasta.)

4. Toss the pasta gently with the crab-cream mixture.

5. Divide into four pasta bowls and serve immediately.

ONE SERVING: 390 Calories; 13.7 grams Fat (5.2 Saturated); 135 mg Cholesterol.

IN A HURRY? For an even quicker dish, use vacuum packed fresh lump crabmeat. Dried linguine may be substituted for the fresh—just adjust the cooking time. If Pommery mustard is not available, substitute any grainy mustard.

HEALTH TIP: For an even lighter dish, evaporated skim milk can be substituted for the cream. However, the half-and-half (1/4 cup per serving) in this dish weighs in with a respectable 78 calories, 7.0 grams of fat, and 22 milligrams of cholesterol.

MAKE AHEAD: The sauce
may be made in advance
and reheated briefly in a
microwave before combin-
ing it with the pasta.

VARIATION: The sauce is
delicious served on quar-
tered baked potatoes.

ITALIAN RED PEPPER PESTO

Chef Phillip McGuire's way of leaving the charred skin on
roasted peppers gives this dish an intriguing smokey taste.
Serve it as a first course, a vegetarian entree, or a delectable
accompaniment to grilled fish.

4 Servings
Preparation Time: 25 minutes

4 red bell peppers
4 cloves garlic, peeled
1 cup freshly grated
   parmesan cheese
2 tbsp. olive oil

⅛ tsp. salt
freshly ground pepper to
   taste
12 oz. fettucine, cooked
   and drained

1. Preheat grill or oven to 450 degrees.

2. Roast the peppers over a grill until most of the skin is
charred; or place peppers on a baking sheet and roast in the
preheated oven, turning every 5 minutes, for about 15 minutes. When cool enough to handle, cut each pepper in half
and remove the core and seeds. Don't worry about removing
the charred skin; it adds a nice smoky flavor. Coarsely chop
the pepper.

3. In a food processor, purée the garlic briefly. Add the peppers, cheese, and olive oil along with the salt and pepper.
Purée for 15 to 20 seconds. Taste and add more salt if
needed.

4. Toss the sauce with hot, drained fettucine and serve immediately. Top each portion with freshly ground pepper.

ONE SERVING: 248 Calories; 13.6 grams Fat; 15 mg Cholesterol.

ANGEL HAIR PASTA WITH CHICKEN, BASIL, AND OLIVES

Rejoice fresh herb lovers! This sauce from Robert Casella is filled with all the herbal essence that makes Italian cooking so satisfying—for only 321 calories per serving. The restaurant in San Francisco that featured the talents of Chef Casella is no longer open, but this recipe is ours to savor.

4 Servings
Preparation Time: 20 minutes
Cooking Time: 20 minutes

1 lb. boneless chicken breasts, cut into 1-inch cubes
1 tbsp. olive oil
1 clove garlic, minced
2 tsp. chopped fresh thyme
2 tsp. chopped fresh oregano
2 tsp. chopped fresh marjoram
½ lb. mushrooms, sliced
1 large tomato, chopped
½ cup chicken broth
¼ cup dry white wine
½ tsp. ground pepper
2 tbsp. freshly grated parmesan cheese
2 tbsp. chopped oil-cured olives
2 tbsp. chopped fresh basil
salt and freshly ground pepper to taste
1 lb. angel hair pasta, cooked and drained
fresh basil leaves for garnish

1. In a large, heavy skillet sauté chicken in olive oil until brown, about 5 minutes. Remove and keep warm.

2. Add garlic, thyme, oregano, and marjoram to the skillet and cook, stirring, over low heat for one minute. Add mushrooms, tomato, broth, and wine. Cook uncovered over medium heat for about 10 minutes, stirring occasionally. Add parmesan cheese, olives, chopped basil, salt, and pepper. Cook and stir until cheese melts.

3. To serve, toss the chicken and sauce gently with the pasta and garnish with fresh basil leaves.

ONE SERVING: 321 Calories; 10.3 grams Fat (2.3 Saturated); 73 mg Cholesterol.

HINT: Using fresh, flavorful oil-cured olives from the deli makes this dish special. Greek Calamata olives are salty and have a distinct pungent taste. The huge, dark olive from Italy called Alfonso would also be delightful; or substitute the milder, water-packed canned black olives.

MAKE AHEAD: This dish may be prepared ahead of time up through Step Two, then refrigerated. Bring it to room temperature before reheating and tossing with the pasta.

HINT: *To protect yourself from the stinging oils, always wear gloves when handling hot peppers.*

HEALTH TIP: *Turkey bacon can be substituted to lower calorie and fat content.*

RIGATONI WITH APPLES AND BACON IN A PEPPERED VODKA SAUCE

The Russian Tea Room is often filled with New York City celebrities enjoying the fabulous creations of Chef Anthony Damiano.

6 Servings
Preparation Time: 20 minutes
Cooking Time: 20 minutes

1½ lb. rigatoni
12 oz. lean bacon, diced
1 small peeled and cored apple, finely chopped
2 tbsp. chopped garlic
2 jalapeno peppers, seeded and finely chopped

3 tbsp. vodka (or pepper flavored vodka)
3 cups tomato sauce (or bottled marinara sauce)
cayenne pepper (optional)

1. Cook pasta according to package directions. Drain. Mix with a little of the tomato sauce to keep moist. Cover and set aside.

2. In a large, heavy saucepan sauté the bacon and apples until the bacon is done, about 5 minutes. Drain excess fat, then add the garlic and peppers. Cook, stirring, for 1 or 2 minutes.

3. Add the vodka and stir. Add the tomato sauce and heat thoroughly.

4. Toss the hot sauce with the pasta. Taste for seasoning. Add cayenne pepper for more spice. Serve immediately.

ONE SERVING: 252 Calories; 5.5 grams Fat; 32 mg Cholesterol.

PASTA WITH SUNDRIED AND FRESH TOMATO SAUCE

The Clevenger family—owner JoAnn and her son Jason, a sous chef—and executive chef, Tom Cowman, are creating a culinary sensation at the Upperline restaurant in New Orleans. *Gourmet* magazine reports, "The Upperline has a terrific touch with pasta!" Try this signature dish and you can taste for yourself!

6 Servings
Preparation Time: 1 hour

⅓ cup water
⅓ cup red wine
⅓ cup white wine
4½ tbsp. olive oil
½ cup sundried tomatoes
2 shallots, minced
3 tbsp. chopped fresh basil
1 clove garlic, minced
1 bay leaf
1 cup skim milk

freshly ground black pepper
8 ripe tomatoes, peeled, seeded, and coarsely chopped
1 tsp. sugar
4 tbsp. finely chopped parsley
4 tbsp. balsamic vinegar
salt to taste
1¼ lb. fettucini, cooked al dente and drained

1. In a saucepan, bring water, red wine, white wine, and ½ tablespoon olive oil to a boil. Remove from heat and marinate sundried tomatoes in the mixture until cool.

2. In a saucepan, cook ½ cup drained marinated tomatoes, shallots, 1 tablespoon basil, garlic, and bay leaf until all vegetables are soft and tender. Stir in milk and cook over medium heat until mixture is reduced by half. Remove, place in blender, blend until smooth, then strain. Return to saucepan and reduce until the sauce has the consistency of heavy cream.

HINT: For maximum flavor, refrigerate the marinated tomatoes for two days before using them.

3. In a large bowl, combine chopped ripe tomatoes, sugar, parsley, vinegar, and the remaining 4 tablespoons olive oil and 2 tablespoons basil. Salt and pepper to taste; then add the sundried tomato sauce and mix thoroughly. Serve over cooked fettucini.

ONE SERVING: 240 Calories; 11.7 grams Fat (2.2 Saturated); 4 mg Cholesterol.

PASTA WITH SMOKED SALMON AND DILL

At the restaurant, By Word of Mouth, in Ft. Lauderdale, Florida, Chef James Caron serves this sophisticated pasta course in a clear glass bowl. The taste is worthy of your finest crystal.

6 Servings
Preparation Time: 30 minutes

1 lb. fusilli pasta
1 cup olive oil
½ cup white wine vinegar
3 cloves garlic, peeled
½ cup minced fresh dill
1¾ tsp. salt

1½ tsp. black pepper
½ lb. smoked salmon, cut into strips
¼ cup salmon roe caviar (or 2 oz. beluga)
fresh dill for garnish

1. Cook pasta in boiling water until just tender. Drain and allow to cool.

2. In a food processor, combine olive oil, vinegar, garlic, dill, salt, and pepper; blend well. Pour into a bowl and add salmon and caviar. Toss with pasta and garnish with fresh dill.

ONE SERVING: 404 Calories; 32.0 grams Fat (4.1 Saturated); 113 mg Cholesterol.

NICE WITH: A starter salad of bibb lettuce, shredded carrots, and minced onions drizzled with a creamy dressing (made of yogurt, low-fat mayonnaise, herbs, and black pepper whisked together); whole grain rolls; and iced tea with lemon.

IN A HURRY? Too tired or weak-of-wallet to prepare this caviar-salmon delight? Bring home a prepared smoked-salmon spread from a superior deli and toss it with fresh cooked pasta for a very attractive and quick dinner.

PASTA WITH GOAT CHEESE, TOMATO, AND CUCUMBERS

The succhietto that Chef Steven Hunn uses for this specialty is a corkscrew pasta with holes. If you can't find it, fuselli will combine just as well with the summer vegetables and vinaigrette.

4 Servings
Preparation Time: 20 minutes
Chilling Time: At least one hour

1 lb. succhietto pasta
3 tbsp. olive oil
2 cucumbers, peeled, halved, seeded, and thinly sliced
2 tomatoes, quartered, seeded, and julienned
1 tsp. snipped chives

2 tbsp. sherry wine vinegar
freshly ground pepper
4 cups mixed leafy garden lettuce
4 oz. goat cheese, crumbled

1. Cook the pasta according to package directions. Drain, then toss with 1 tablespoon olive oil. Place in a bowl covered with a damp cloth and chill in the refrigerator for at least one hour.

2. In a large bowl, toss the chilled pasta with cucumbers, tomatoes, chives, vinegar, and remaining 2 tablespoons olive oil. Add ground pepper to taste. Arrange lettuce on serving plates, top with pasta, and sprinkle with the goat cheese.

ONE SERVING: 193 Calories; 16.8 grams Fat (5.7 Saturated); 24 mg Cholesterol.

HEALTH TIP: How fortunate we are to have a such a variety of chèvre—fresh, tangy goat cheese! Lower in fat than most cheeses, goat cheese can be used in every aspect of cooking. Look for aged goat cheese, which can be used in the place of parmesan; buttery Boucheron from France; or creamy Montrachet, which spreads deliciously on apple slices.

BANGKOK PASTA

An intriguing toss of creamy, spicy ingredients. "Perfect," says Chef Robert Maxwell, "if you can't decide which you love the most—pasta or Thai food." Chef Maxwell, who prepares elaborate floating feasts for guests on charter yachts, says this is a dish he often cooks for himself when he has a chance to relax at home—which happens to also be a boat!

4 Servings
Preparation Time: 15 minutes
Cooking Time: 10 minutes

8 oz. angel hair pasta
1 tbsp. vegetable oil
1 small onion, finely chopped
6 scallions, slivered with green and white pieces separated
2 tbsp. shredded fresh ginger
½ cup white wine
½ cup low-calorie mayonnaise

1 tbsp. red chili paste
1 tbsp. all-fruit apricot jam
1 tbsp. lemon juice
8 oz. cooked pork roast, trimmed of fat and cut in slivers
¼ cup low-salt, dry-roasted peanuts, chopped fine
freshly ground pepper

1. Place pasta and a dash of salt in a large pot of boiling water. Stir and remove from heat.

2. In a heavy skillet, heat vegetable oil over moderate heat. Sauté onion, white scallion pieces, and ginger for 2 minutes. Stir in wine, then turn off heat and stir in mayonnaise, chili paste, jam, and lemon juice. Add pork strips, peanuts, green onion slivers, and freshly ground pepper. Mix thoroughly.

3. Drain pasta. Toss lightly with the sauce and serve.

ONE SERVING: 465 Calories; 20 grams Fat (4.3 Saturated); 54 mg Cholesterol.

ZITI ITALIANO

This is another good-for-you concoction from Chef Robert Casella. Put some Italian bread sticks on the table, open a bottle of Chianti, and turn the music to Verdi. *Buon Appetito!*

4 Servings
Preparation Time: 15 minutes
Cooking Time: 45 minutes

2 tsp. olive oil	1 cup canned tomatoes
2 cloves garlic, minced	3 tbsp. tomato paste
½ cup chopped onion	½ cup red wine
½ cup diced carrot	½ tsp. salt
½ cup diced fresh fennel bulb	⅛ tsp. freshly ground pepper
¾ lb. ground lean turkey	⅛ tsp. ground red pepper (optional)
1 tbsp. paprika	12 oz. dry ziti
1 tsp. dried oregano	chopped fennel leaves for garnish
1 tsp. dried basil	
1 cup sliced fresh mushrooms	

1. In a large, heavy saucepan, heat oil over medium heat. Add garlic, onion, carrot, and fennel. Cook, stirring, for 2 to 3 minutes.

2. Add turkey and cook, stirring, until turkey is no longer pink, about 4 minutes. Add paprika, oregano, and basil, mixing thoroughly. Add mushrooms, and cook for 2 minutes. Stir in tomatoes, tomato paste, red wine, salt, black pepper, and red pepper. Simmer for 30 minutes, stirring occasionally.

3. Meanwhile, cook ziti according to package directions. Drain.

4. Toss ziti with sauce. Garnish with chopped fennel leaves and serve.

ONE SERVING: 444 Calories; 15.15 grams Fat (6.1 Saturated); 72 mg Cholesterol.

HINT: As Chef Casella does in this recipe, always add dried spices to ground turkey while it is being sautéed. Cook and stir thoroughly before adding liquid. The meat will have a more appealing color and much more flavor.

HEALTH TIP: When purchasing ground turkey, make sure you are buying meat that has been ground without skin. Half of the fat calories of any poultry meat is found in the skin.

VARIATION: If a specialty pasta shop is available, flavored cappellini (garlic or herb) is a nice substitution. The thin strands of cappellini pasta are slightly thicker than capelli (angel hair) pasta. Cappellini cooks in two to four minutes.

MAKE AHEAD: Make herb broth up to two days in advance and refrigerate.

IN A HURRY? Grill the baby vegetables along with the swordfish. Serve with cappellini that has been tossed with chopped tomatoes and fresh herbs.

CAPPELLINI WITH GRILLED SWORDFISH, BABY VEGETABLES, AND HERB BROTH

This is the enlightened sort of cooking that one expects from a great contemporary chef like Michael Powers of California Cafe in Corte Madera.

4 Servings
Preparation Time: 3 hours

1 bulb fennel	2 bunches tarragon
2 bulbs garlic, separated into cloves and peeled	2 bunches oregano
	salt and pepper
2 carrots	3 oz. baby yellow squash
1 head celery	8 baby carrots, peeled, with tops
3 medium onions	4 6-oz. swordfish steaks
2 bell peppers	1 lb. cappellini pasta
2 bunches parsley	4 oz. chopped tomato for garnish
2 bunches thyme	

1. Preheat oven to 350 degrees.

2. Coarsely chop fennel, garlic, carrots, celery, onions, peppers, and herbs. Place in a foil-lined baking pan and roast in preheated oven until dark brown but not burned, about 20 minutes. Place roasted vegetables and herbs in a stock pot, cover with water, and simmer for 2 hours. Season to taste with salt and pepper. Strain out the vegetables and return herb broth to pot.

3. Bring herb broth to a simmer.

4. When ready to serve, bring 3 quarts salted water to a boil in a large pot. Place baby squash and carrots in boiling water briefly to blanche; then add them to the herb broth.

5. Meanwhile, grill the swordfish for approximately 3 minutes on each side.

6. Place cappellini in the boiling water, cook 2 minutes, then drain. Then place pasta in Herb Broth and stir.

7. Place pasta in bowls. Arrange baby vegetables around bowl. Pour in herb broth, then lay grilled swordfish on pasta. Top with chopped tomato.

ONE SERVING: 273 Calories; 5.0 grams Fat (0.9 Saturated); 75 mg Cholesterol.

ARTICHOKE RAVIOLI
WITH TOMATO COMPOTE

Compliments are guaranteed if you take the time to make this knockout ravioli dish from the Four Seasons in Philadelphia. Chef Lacroix says to use your imagination when cutting ravioli—try squares, half moons, etc. Garnish it with your choice of the freshest vegetables you can find.

6 Servings
Preparation Time: 2 hours (less if pasta machine is used)

Ravioli:

10 artichokes
3 tsp. olive oil
3 shallots, finely chopped
3 cloves garlic, finely
 chopped
5 tomatoes, diced
3 sprigs parsley
salt and pepper
4 eggs
1 lb. flour
¼ cup plus 2 tbsp. water

Tomato Compote and Garnish:

10 tomatoes, blanched,
 peeled, and seeded
1 sprig thyme
5 whole cloves garlic
12 snow peas, blanced
3 yellow squash, halved,
 sliced, and blanched
mushrooms, sliced and
 briefly sautéed

IN A HURRY? If you have access to a pasta machine, make sheets of pasta and cut the time requirement for this recipe in half.

1. Cook artichokes until tender in lightly salted water for about 30 to 40 minutes. Remove and allow to cool. When cool enough to handle, peel and discard all but the centers. Coarsely chop artichoke meat.

2. In a large skillet, heat 2 teaspoons of the oil, and slowly cook the shallots, garlic, tomatoes, parsley, and chopped artichoke until all vegetables are tender and moist, about 5 minutes. Season to taste with salt and pepper.

3. Combine three eggs, flour, ¼ cup water, and remaining teaspoon of olive oil. Knead dough twice, allowing it to rest in refrigerator for 20 minutes between kneading.

4. Roll dough to ⅛-inch thickness. Cut ravioli into 3-inch rounds.

5. Assemble ravioli by placing 1 tablespoon artichoke mixture in the middle of pasta rounds. Combine remaining egg with 2 tablespoons of water to make an egg wash. Brush inside edges of pasta with egg wash and crimp. Place filled ravioli in boiling, salted water for 1 minute.

6. To make the compote, roughly chop the tomatoes. In a large saucepan, cook tomatoes with thyme and garlic until mixture is almost dry; then remove garlic and thyme.

7. Place 2 tablespoons of tomato compote in the center of each serving plate and top with ravioli. Garnish with snow peas, squash, and mushrooms. Serve.

ONE SERVING: 282 Calories; 6.2 grams Fat; 0 mg Cholesterol.

UDON NOODLE, SHITAKE MUSHROOM, AND GREEN ONION PANCAKE WITH PEANUT-MISO SAUCE

If you enjoy udon noodles in a soup bowl, wait until you try these cakes designed by Unicorn Village's chef, Steven Petusevsky.

4 Servings
Preparation Time: 25 minutes

Pancake:

1 lb. fresh udon noodles
    (6 oz. dry)
1 tsp. sesame oil
1 cup thinly sliced
    shitake mushrooms,
    stems removed
3 scallions, minced
½ cup minced water
    chestnuts
1 tsp. minced fresh ginger
1 tsp. minced fresh garlic
4 oz. tamari or soy sauce
1 oz. arrowroot (or
    cornstarch)

1 cup dried bread crumbs
canola oil (or vegetable
    oil)

Peanut-Miso Sauce:

8 oz. peanut butter
1 tsp. fresh minced ginger
1 tsp. fresh minced garlic
1 tbsp. white mellow miso
2 oz. tamari or soy sauce
2 tbsp. brown rice syrup
2 oz. lime or lemon juice
1 tbsp. red chili flakes
water

1. After cooking Udon noodles according to package directions, cut them into 2-inch pieces.

2. In a skillet, add sesame oil and mushrooms. Sauté lightly, then remove from heat.

3. In a large bowl, mix together the noodles, mushrooms, scallions, water chestnuts, ginger, garlic, soy sauce, arrowroot, and ½ of the bread crumbs. If the mixture is not thick enough to form pancakes, add the remaining bread crumbs.

4. Form into 3-ounce pancakes, flattening with the palm of your hand. Set aside.

MAKE AHEAD: Pancakes may be made up through Step Four and refrigerated for up to eight hours before sautéing.

NOTE: Udon noodles are a thick, white wheat noodle. Fresh udon noodles are called nama udon. The dried variety look like long, flat sticks and are sold in boxes at Japanese markets and some specialty food stores. The fresh noodles cook in boiling water for three minutes; dried for ten minutes. Rinse in cold water and drain. Any ribbon pasta can be substituted for the udon noodles.

HEALTH TIP: Miso, also called bean paste, is a basic flavoring in much of Japanese cooking. It has abundant amounts of B vitamins and protein and is easily digested. Chef Petusevsky prefers to use the pale, mellow variety. Miso can be found in Japanese markets and health food stores, as can the brown rice syrup used in this recipe.

5. Brush a non-stick pan with vegetable oil and place over high heat until hot. Add pancakes. Do not overcrowd the pan. Sauté pancakes until golden brown, 3 or 4 minutes on each side.

6. Mix first 8 sauce ingredients together, then add enough water to thin sauce to desired consistency. Mix thoroughly.

7. Pour sauce over pancakes and serve.

ONE SERVING: 466 Calories; 29 grams Fat (4.6 Saturated); 0 mg Cholesterol.

TORTELLONI KAHALA

Chef Dominique Jamain has given us total indulgence— creamy pasta tossed with nuts, herbs, shitakes, chicken, and wine—with fewer than 500 calories. The award-winning Maile Restaurant at the Kahala Hilton in Honolulu is one of only 15 restaurants in the United States to win the American Automobile Association's Five Diamond Award. Additionally, Maile was voted "Restaurant of the Year" by readers of *Honolulu* magazine.

6 Servings
Preparation and Cooking Time: 1 hour

4 cups chicken stock
2 cloves garlic, peeled
8 shallots, minced
6 fresh basil leaves, minced
2 tbsp. half-and-half
1 tbsp. cornstarch
2 tbsp. water
salt and pepper
¾ lb. tortelloni pasta
2½ tbsp. olive oil
8 oz. skinless chicken breasts, in very thin strips

1 cup thinly sliced shitake mushrooms, stems removed
2 oz. Marsala wine
juice of ½ lemon
2 small tomatoes, peeled, seeded, and cut into small strips
½ cup finely chopped basil
4 oil-cured olives, cut into small strips
2 tbsp. roasted pine nuts
¼ cup grated parmesan cheese (optional)

NOTE: *Tortelloni is a larger version of the more familiar tortellini—which can be substituted. Either pasta can be purchased stuffed with meat, cheese, or vegetables.*

HINT: *Toast the pine nuts by quickly shaking in the hot skillet before adding oil and continuing with Step Four.*

1. In a saucepan over medium-high heat, combine chicken stock, garlic, ½ of the shallots and the 6 minced basil leaves. Cook until mixture is reduced to about 1½ cups of liquid. Add half-and-half. Cook for 3 minutes. Mix together cornstarch and water; then add it to the sauce. Simmer for 2 to 3 minutes, stirring constantly to make a smooth, thick sauce. Remove from heat and cool slightly.

2. In a blender, blend the sauce in small batches until smooth. Taste for seasonings and add salt and pepper to taste. Strain and keep warm.

3. Meanwhile, cook pasta in boiling water along with ½ tablespoon of olive oil and a little salt for about 7 to 8 minutes. Do not overcook. Drain, but do not rinse the pasta.

4. Just before serving, heat a large, non-stick skillet until it is very hot. Add the remaining 2 tablespoons of olive oil, then immediately add chicken strips and sauté for 1 to 2 minutes. Add shitakes and remaining ½ of the shallots and toss with the chicken. Add wine and lemon juice, then cook until almost all liquid has evaporated.

5. In a large bowl, combine contents of skillet with the pasta, sauce, tomatoes, and ¼ cup of the chopped basil. Toss. Serve immediately garnished with olive strips, pine nuts, the remaining basil, and parmesan cheese.

ONE SERVING (With cheese-filled tortelloni): 492 Calories; 23.8 grams Fat (8.9 Saturated); 189 mg Cholesterol.

Fish
and
Seafood

Fish and Seafood

Herb-Crusted Codfish in Rosemary Vinaigrette

Roasted Swordfish with Olives and Leeks

Pan-Seared Tuna Steak with Lobster and
Fresh Fennel Sauce

Red Snapper with Golden Tomato Salsa

Roasted Smoked Halibut with Braised Cabbage
and Parsleyed Potatoes

Portuguese Swordfish

Monkfish Medallions with Asparagus, Morels, and Madeira

Braised Redfish

Poached Salmon with Dilled Cucumber Sauce

Salmon with Tomato and Chives

Grilled Salmon with Fresh Corn and Tomato Salsa

Pan-Seared Swordfish with Toasted Rice Sauce

Fillet of Sole Picasso

Grilled Tuna on Roasted Vegetables
with Pineapple-Soy Vinaigrette

Baked Gulf Fish with Horseradish Crust

Mahimahi Oporto

Broiled Fillet of Pacific Halibut with Cilantro-Artichoke Relish

Bon Ton Cafe's Crabmeat Imperial

Dry-Fried Shrimp with Roasted Shallots

Tuna Decatur

Baked Eggplant with Seafood

Grilled Lobster and Scallop Kebobs

Shrimp Creole

Sea Scallop Sauté with Black Bean and Chipotle Stew

Sweet Corn Sauce for Seafood

Swordfish in Mustard Seed Crust

NICE WITH: Coleslaw made with cabbage, peppers, onions, carrots and low-fat mayonnaise.

MAKE AHEAD: Prepare Rosemary Oil at least 2 days ahead for flavors to develop. Store any unused oil in the refrigerator. The dish itself may be prepared through Step Three and refrigerated.

HEALTH TIP: Cod has one of the lowest fat and calorie counts of any fish.

HERB-CRUSTED CODFISH IN ROSEMARY VINAIGRETTE

At Le Bernardin in New York City, Chef Eberhard Müller turns ho-hum cod into one of the best fish dishes ever tasted—low-cal or otherwise.

4 Servings
Preparation Time: 30 minutes
Cooking Time: 15 minutes

4 tbsp. Rosemary Oil (see recipe) or extra virgin olive oil
½ tbsp. plus 1½ tsp. finely chopped shallot or white part of scallion
¾ tsp. minced garlic
1½ tsp. finely chopped fresh rosemary
¼ tsp. finely chopped fresh thyme
1 1-inch bay leaf
⅓ cup dry white wine
¼ cup fish stock or chicken broth
1 tbsp. fresh lemon juice
½ tbsp. plus 1 tsp. finely chopped fresh parsley
¾ cup French bread crumbs
¼ tsp. salt
¼ tsp. pepper
1 large egg
1 tbsp. water
¼ cup flour
4 5-oz. codfish fillets (1¼ inches thick)
1 tbsp. olive oil

1. In a skillet, heat 2 tablespoons Rosemary Oil. Add ½ tablespoon shallot and ¼ teaspoon garlic; then cook over medium-low heat for 3 to 5 minutes, stirring occasionally. Add ½ teaspoon rosemary and the thyme, bay leaf, wine, and stock. Increase heat to medium-high and boil for 2 to 3 minutes until about half the liquid has evaporated. Stir in remaining 2 tablespoons Rosemary Oil and the lemon juice. Cover and keep vinaigrette warm over very low heat.

2. In a small bowl, combine the bread crumbs, salt, and pepper with the remaining 1½ teaspoons shallot, ½ teaspoon garlic, 1 teaspoon rosemary, and 1 teaspoon parsley. In another small bowl, beat egg with 1 tablespoon water. Spread flour in a flat dish or on waxed paper.

3. Dip only one side of each fish fillet in flour, then egg mixture, then bread crumb mixture to coat.

4. In a large, heavy skillet, warm 1 tablespoon olive oil over low heat. Oil should not get hot. Place fillets, crumb side down, in pan and cook over low heat for 8 to 10 minutes, until crumbs are golden and the fish is almost opaque (top will look translucent). Turn over and continue cooking over low heat for 3 to 5 minutes until fish is opaque in center when tested with tip of knife.

5. Remove bay leaf from vinaigrette. Stir in remaining chopped parsley.

6. To serve, place fish on serving plate. Spoon warm vinaigrette around fish.

ONE SERVING: 380 Calories; 24 grams Fat (4.9 Saturated); 114 mg Cholesterol.

Rosemary Oil:

1 cup olive oil
2 6-inch sprigs fresh
    rosemary
1 3-inch sprig fresh
    thyme

1 small clove garlic,
    peeled
6 whole black
    peppercorns
1 1½-inch bay leaf

1. In a small saucepan, heat all ingredients until hot. Reduce heat to low and heat for 30 minutes so flavors can permeate oil.

2. Allow to cool, then pour into a wide-mouth jar. Cover tightly and refrigerate.

PER TABLESPOON: 120 Calories; 12 grams Fat; 0 mg Cholesterol.

ROASTED SWORDFISH WITH OLIVES AND LEEKS

Of the 4-Star Everest Room, the restaurant critic of the *Chicago Tribune* wrote, "The place is magnificent, a temple of food in which Chef Jean Joho, arguably the most creative chef in the area, masterfully holds sway." Try this oven-poached fish with its harmonious sauce, and see why Jean Joho is one of the most famous chefs in America.

4 Servings
Preparation and Cooking Time: 30 minutes

2 tsp. olive oil
4 4½-oz. swordfish
   steaks
8 green olives, diced
8 black olives, diced
½ cup chopped green
   onions
¼ cup seeded, chopped
   red bell pepper
¼ cup chopped parsley
¼ cup chopped basil
juice of 8 tomatoes
juice of one lemon
2 cups braised julienne of
   leeks

1. Preheat the oven to 425 degrees.

2. Oil a 9 x 12 inch baking pan with olive oil and place swordfish on it. Sprinkle olives, onions, red pepper, parsley, and basil over the fish. Pour the tomato and lemon juices over the fish, making sure the fish is covered with liquid.

3. Place baking pan on stove and bring liquid to a simmer.

4. Place the pan in a 425-degree oven until swordfish is done, about 4-6 minutes. Serve the swordfish topped with the remaining juices and the braised leeks.

ONE SERVING: 234 Calories; 8.1 grams Fat (1.4 Saturated); 66 mg Cholesterol.

PAN SEARED TUNA STEAK WITH LOBSTER AND FRESH FENNEL SAUCE

If you are a fennel lover—or about to become one—-this simple-to-prepare dish is for you. It comes from The Occidental in Washington, D.C., which has won the Conde Naste Distinguished Restaurant Award.

4 servings
Preparation Time: 15 minutes
Cooking Time: 15 minutes

2 tbsp. olive oil
3 shallots, minced
2 garlic cloves, minced
2 tbsp. finely chopped fresh fennel bulb
1½ tsp. anise seed
4 oz. dry white wine
1 pinch saffron
4 ripe tomatoes, finely chopped
8 oz. strong chicken or fish stock

salt and freshly ground pepper
2 tsp. fennel seeds
1 tsp. fresh or dried thyme
4 6-oz. thick-cut tuna steaks, fat, skin, and dark portion removed
8 oz. cooked lobster meat or shrimp, diced
2 tsp. chopped fennel leaves

1. In a medium saucepan, heat 1 tablespoon olive oil. Add shallots, garlic, chopped fennel bulb, and ½ teaspoon anise seed. Sauté, stirring constantly, for 1 to 2 minutes. Add white wine and saffron and cook until volume is reduced by half. Add tomatoes and stock. Simmer for 7 to 8 minutes and correct seasoning with salt and pepper.

2. Crush the fennel seeds (see NOTE). Combine with thyme. Coat tuna steaks with the spice mixture.

3. In a very hot skillet, heat 1 tablespoon olive oil. Sear the tuna until golden brown on each side, about 6 minutes.

4. To serve, add the lobster and chopped fennel leaves to the fennel sauce. Spoon sauce over tuna steaks.

ONE SERVING: 336 Calories; 6.4 grams Fat (1.6 Saturated); 99 mg Cholesterol.

If basil was the herb of the eighties, fennel is a strong contender for the herb of the nineties. The crunchy texture and mild licorice taste of the fresh fennel bulb adds a new note to a myriad of sauces and vegetables mixtures.

NOTE: Fennel seeds may be crushed using a mortar and pestle, or placed on cutting board and crushed with the bottom of a heavy skillet.

RED SNAPPER WITH GOLDEN TOMATO SALSA

This is a breeze to prepare and a sensation on the palate! It is yet another winner from Routh Street Cafe's Chef Stephan Pyles.

4 Servings
Preparation Time: 20 minutes
Cooking Time: 8 minutes

1 lb. ripe yellow
   tomatoes, diced
2 tbsp. diced red bell
   pepper
2 tbsp. diced green bell
   pepper
2 tbsp. diced yellow bell
   pepper
2 tbsp. diced chives
2 serrano chilies, seeds
   and ribs removed,
   minced

1 tbsp. fruit-flavored
   vinegar
1 tbsp. lime juice
1 tbsp. chopped cilantro
salt and freshly ground
   black pepper
4 6-oz. red snapper fillets,
   1 inch at the thickest
   part
flour
2 tbsp. olive oil

1. To make the salsa, combine the first nine ingredients in a large bowl. Add salt and pepper to taste and set aside.

2. Season fish on both sides with salt and pepper. Dredge lightly with flour. In a skillet, heat oil until lightly smoking. Sauté fish for 2 to 3 minutes on each side.

3. Serve with salsa that has been slightly warmed.

ONE SERVING (With ¼ cup salsa): 424 Calories; 24.5 grams Fat (3.8 Saturated); 94 mg Cholesterol.

ROASTED SMOKED HALIBUT WITH BRAISED CABBAGE AND PARSLEYED POTATOES

Truffles at Casa Ybel on Sanibel Island was chosen "Best New Restaurant in Florida" by *Gulf Shore* magazine. Chef Michael Jacob's menu features southwestern and Caribbean cuisine. Use Garlic-Chive Oil and Lemon-Basil Oil on the halibut—or make it faster by substituting extra-virgin olive oil—either way this is stylish food for fish lovers.

6 Servings
Marinate: 4 hours
Cooking Time: 35 minutes

6 6-oz. halibut steaks, skin and bones removed	4 tbsp. Lemon-Basil Oil (see recipe)
5 to 6 tbsp. Garlic-Chive Oil (see recipe)	salt and pepper
2 shallots, minced	12 small new potatoes, boiled
1 lb. Savoy or green cabbage, sliced	2 tbsp. chopped parsley
2 cups shrimp or seafood stock	4 sprigs parsley for garnish

1. Marinate halibut in 4 tablespoons Garlic-Chive Oil for 4 hours.

2. Remove fish from marinade, drain, and place in smoker for 2 minutes on each side. Remove.

3. In a large, heavy saucepan over medium heat, heat 1 teaspoon Garlic-Chive Oil. Add shallots and sauté until soft, but not brown. Add cabbage and sauté until wilted. Add 1 cup stock and simmer until cabbage is barely tender, about 5 minutes.

IN A HURRY? Bottled clam juice can be substituted for seafood stock, you may bypass smoking the fish, or use plain extra virgin olive oil instead of the flavored oils. According to Chef Jacobs, "the flavor will be changed slightly, but it will still be delicious."

MAKE AHEAD: Halibut steaks may be refrigerated for several hours after Step Two.

4. Heat a large, heavy-bottomed skillet over medium heat. Add 2 tablespoons Lemon-Basil Oil, then add halibut and lightly brown on each side. (Be careful not to overcook fish. It should be medium to medium-rare.) Place halibut on cutting board.

5. Deglaze skillet with remaining 1 cup seafood stock. Add cabbage mixture and cook until barely tender. Toss with 2 tablespoons of Lemon-Basil Oil, and salt and pepper to taste.

6. To serve, place cabbage with sauce on plate. Slice halibut into bite-sized pieces and place of top of cabbage. Serve with boiled potatoes which have been tossed in a bit of Garlic-Chive Oil (optional) and chopped parsley. Garnish with parsley sprigs.

ONE SERVING (With vegetables): 497 Calories; 29.7 grams Fat (5.5 Saturated); 84 mg Cholesterol.

Garlic-Chive Oil:

1 cup extra virgin olive oil	2 oz. chives, in 1-inch
6 cloves crushed garlic	pieces

Combine ingredients, and store in a warm place for 1 week.

Lemon-Basil Oil:

1 cup extra virgin olive oil	1 oz. fresh basil
juice of one lemon	

Combine ingredients and store in a warm place for 1 week. (Above the stove top is ideal).

PORTUGUESE SWORDFISH

Grilled fish with a vegetable-saffron topping—healthy eating for hearty appetites—with less than 250 calories, from the creative kitchen of The Barrows House. Chef Tim Blackwell serves dinner to the public as well as the guests of The Barrows House, an elegant country inn set in a historic building in the quiet rural village of Dorset, Vermont.

4 Servings
Preparation Time: 15 minutes
Cooking Time: 30 minutes

½ cup lemon juice
pinch saffron
1 tsp. cumin
1 cup water
¾ cup finely diced
    Spanish onion
½ cup finely diced celery
½ cup sliced carrot

6 new potatoes, quartered
1 large tomato, finely
    diced
1 bay leaf
4 5-oz. swordfish steaks
1 tbsp. vegetable oil
dash cayenne pepper
dash black pepper

1. Preheat grill.

2. In a small bowl, combine lemon juice, saffron, and cumin.

3. In a large saucepan, combine water, onion, celery, carrot, potatoes, tomato, and bay leaf. Bring to a boil; then reduce heat and simmer until all vegetables are tender, about 20 minutes.

4. Brush swordfish steaks with oil and sprinkle with peppers. Grill to desired doneness, about 4 minutes on each side.

5. Serve swordfish on vegetable-saffron mixture.

ONE SERVING: 232 Calories; 7.8 grams Fat (1.4 Saturated); 56 mg Cholesterol.

NICE WITH: Red wine with fish? Certainly. A fruity Beaujolais would be delightful with this hearty tomato sauced dish.

NICE WITH: *Oven-roasted new potatoes, broiled tomato halves, and a big glass of Chardonnay.*

MONKFISH MEDALLIONS WITH ASPARAGUS, MORELS, AND MADEIRA

John Clancy's was the first restaurant in New York City to serve mesquite-grilled food, but Chef Melissa Lord uses a sauté pan for monkfish—the fish many people say tastes like lobster. The dish is made extra special by an infusion of wine and a quick stir-fry of aromatic vegetables.

4 Servings
Preparation Time: 20 minutes
Cooking Time: 6 minutes

16 dry morel mushrooms
1 cup hot water
flour
1¾ lb. monkfish, in
    ¼-inch slices
3 tbsp. olive oil
½ cup Madeira wine

2 tbsp. minced garlic
4 leeks, julienned
16 asparagus, blanched,
    cut into 1-inch pieces
3 tbsp. minced basil
salt and pepper

1. Soak morels in hot water for 10 minutes. Rinse and trim. Save soaking liquid.

2. Lightly flour monkfish medallions, then shake off excess flour. In a skillet, sauté fish in hot olive oil for 1 minute per side. Pour off excess oil. Deglaze pan with wine.

3. Add garlic, leeks, asparagus, basil, morels, and morel liquid to the skillet. Toss all ingredients to combine flavors. Season with salt and pepper and serve.

ONE SERVING: 283 Calories; 12.8 grams Fat (2.1 Saturated); 71 mg Cholesterol.

BRAISED REDFISH

In Donaldsonville, Louisiana, John Folse was named "1990 National Chef of the Year" for his artistry at Lafitte's Landing restaurant. Not content to merely create a savory fish entree, John Folse sends it to the table with only 120 calories!

4 Servings
Preparation Time: 10 minutes
Marinate: Overnight
Cooking Time: 25 minutes

2 cups bottled oil-free Italian dressing	pinch freshly ground pepper
4 cloves fresh garlic, minced	2 medium onions, sliced
2 tbsp. white wine Worcestershire sauce	1 lb. redfish fillet (or other mild-flavored fish)
juice of 3 lemons	16 green onions, chopped
dash hot sauce	

1. In a bowl, combine Italian dressing, garlic, Worcestershire sauce, lemon juice, hot sauce, and pepper.

2. Line bottom of a shallow baking dish with sliced onions. Place fish over onions and cover with marinade. Refrigerate overnight.

3. Drain all but 1 cup of marinade from baking dish, then cover tightly with foil. Place in a preheated, 350-degree oven for 25 minutes, or until fish flakes when touched.

4. Serve fish on a warm plate with a teaspoon of the braising juices over the top as a glaze. Sprinkle with chopped green onions.

ONE SERVING: 120 Calories; 4.6 grams Fat (0.8 Saturated); 43 mg Cholesterol.

NICE WITH: Rice and salad complete the meal. With such a deliciously low calorie and fat count, you might consider adding a glass of wine. A crisp Sauvignon Blanc with citrus overtones would be lovely.

HEALTH TIP: Braising—a style of cooking meat or fish in a small amount of liquid with no additional fat—is a classic method whose new time has come.

IN A HURRY? Use bottled clam juice instead of the poaching liquid.

HINT: So many fish dishes that are pale in color benefit at serving time by being presented on a black plate. This salmon looks especially pretty alongside bright green beans and boiled new potatoes, set off by a red radish on a gleaming black plate.

POACHED SALMON WITH DILLED CUCUMBER SAUCE

At Penelope's Restaurant Français in Tucson, Arizona, Chef Patricia Sparks brings new-fashioned style and sensibility to an old favorite.

4 Servings
Preparation Time: 15 minutes
Cooking Time: 45 minutes

1½ lb. fish bones
1 onion, chopped
3 bay leaves
2 garlic cloves, chopped
4 parsley sprigs
1 cup dry white wine
3 cups water

1 cup nonfat plain yogurt
4 tbsp. low-fat mayonnaise
2 tbsp. lemon juice
salt and pepper
4 6-oz. salmon fillets

1. In a large saucepan, combine the first 7 ingredients. Bring to a boil, reduce heat, and simmer for 25 to 30 minutes. Strain liquid.

2. In a mixing bowl, combine yogurt, mayonnaise, and lemon juice. Stir to blend well and season to taste with salt and pepper. (The flavors improve if refrigerated for several hours or overnight.)

3. When ready to serve, bring strained poaching liquid to a simmer in a large covered skillet. Add fish, cover, and cook for 8 to 12 minutes, depending on thickness of fish and desired doneness. (Try to keep poaching liquid just below boiling point—this keeps fish moist.) Salmon may be served warm or chilled with cucumber sauce.

ONE SERVING (With ¼ cup sauce): 298 Calories; 13.9 grams Fat (2.7 Saturated); 88 mg Cholesterol.

SALMON WITH TOMATO AND CHIVES

This lovely dish comes from The Wildflower Inn in Vail, Colorado, where apres-skiers sample the culinary magic of Chef Jim Cohen, a James Beard Foundation honoree.

4 Servings
Preparation Time: 10 minutes
Cooking Time: About 25 minutes

4 5-oz. salmon fillets	¼ cup chopped chives
sea salt	1 tbsp. chopped Italian
freshly ground black	parsley
pepper	3 tbsp. Balsamic vinegar
8 tomatoes, peeled,	1 tbsp. Tuscan extra
seeded, and coarsely	virgin olive oil
chopped	(optional)

1. Sprinkle salt and pepper on salmon fillets. Heat a nonstick skillet and place fillets, skin side down, in the skillet. Cover and cook slowly over medium heat until the top of the fish is the only part that looks raw—and it is beginning to slightly change color. The bottom should be crisp.

2. Add tomatoes, cover, cook for 1 minute. Add chives and parsley, then remove from heat and add vinegar. Check tomatoes for seasoning. Add olive oil, if desired.

3. Place fillets on serving plates; then spoon tomato mixture over them and serve.

ONE SERVING: 218 Calories; 9.0 grams Fat (1.6 Saturated); 70 mg Cholesterol.

NICE WITH: Rice pilaf and steamed julienned zucchini.

NOTE: Balsamic vinegar, made in and around Modona, Italy, is valued for its fruity and woody taste. The unfermented juice of the Trebbiano grape is boiled down to a sweet syrup that is aged in wooden barrels. Because of the resulting intense flavor, very little is needed.

HINT: To "score" fish (a criss-cross effect of blackened lines), place on the hot grill at a ninety-degree angle and sear. Turn and repeat. This process works well with thickly cut fish such as salmon, swordfish, mahi-mahi, or snapper.

NICE WITH: Chef Pollack says, "I like to top the hot salmon with a bit of herb or mango butter. Rice and squash, marinated and grilled on a skewer, are delicious accompaniments. Garnish with wedges of lemon and lime."

GRILLED SALMON WITH FRESH CORN AND TOMATO SALSA

At Gypsy Cab Company in St. Augustine, Florida, Chef Nathan Pollack treats fresh salmon to a salsa with no oil or salt—just intense flavor and a riot of color. See for yourself on the cover of this book!

4 Servings
Preparation Time: 30 minutes

1 large ripe tomato, peeled and diced
½ cup fresh raw or frozen corn kernels
1 small red onion, finely chopped
½ cup chopped green pepper
½ cup chopped green onion
2 cloves garlic, minced

jalapeno pepper, minced (to taste)
½ cup fresh lime juice
1 cup tomato sauce
½ bunch fresh cilantro, chopped
chopped fresh oregano (to taste)
1 tbsp. red wine vinegar
4 6-oz. portions fresh salmon

1. Preheat grill.

2. Prepare salsa by combining first twelve ingredients. (It will be even more flavorful if made a day in advance.)

3. Grill salmon to desired doneness, about 4 minutes per side. Serve with the salsa.

ONE SERVING: 238 Calories; 9.0 grams Fat (1.6 Saturated); 70 mg Cholesterol.

Fish and Seafood   107

PAN-SEARED SWORDFISH WITH TOASTED RICE SAUCE

This showstopper from Chef Dean Fearing takes some time—but it will make you famous! Dean Fearing is known to all food savants as the genius in the kitchen at The Mansion on Turtle Creek in Dallas. Both Fearing and the restaurant have garnered just about every imaginable culinary honor.

4 Servings
Preparation and Cooking Time: 1 to 2 hours

¼ cup plus 2 tbsp. uncooked rice
6 large shallots, peeled and chopped
3 cloves garlic, peeled and chopped
2 tbsp. grated fresh ginger
2 scallions, chopped
2 Thai red chilies (or serrano chilies), chopped
¼ cup sweetened rice wine vinegar
¼ cup Thai fish sauce
1 tbsp. chopped fresh cilantro
1½ cups chicken stock
½ red bell pepper, seeds and membranes removed
2 tsp. chopped fresh mint leaves
fresh lime juice to taste
4 6-oz. swordfish steaks, trimmed of fat, skin, and dark membrane
salt
1 tbsp. peanut oil
1 recipe Broccoli-Pickled Eggplant Stir-Fry (see index for recipe) or 2 cups steamed broccoli
¼ cup julienned red bell pepper for garnish

HINT: To pulverize rice in a coffee grinder, grind and discard a few tablespoons of plain rice first to clean the grinder; then continue with instructions.

1. Preheat oven to 350 degrees. Spread uncooked rice on baking sheet and place in preheated oven. Bake for 8 to 10 minutes. Set aside.

2. Place shallots, garlic, ginger, scallions, chilies, rice vinegar, and fish sauce in a medium saucepan. Bring to a boil. Boil for 3 minutes, or until reduced by half. Add ¼ cup browned rice, cilantro, and chicken stock and bring to a boil. Lower heat and simmer until liquid is gone, about 30 minutes. Remove from heat.

3. Pulverize red bell pepper in a food processor, using metal blade. Place in a small piece of cheesecloth and squeeze out all juice. Set pulp aside.

4. Place remaining 2 tablespoons browned rice in a mini coffee grinder and grind until pulverized. (The pulverized brown rice is used as a garnish and is optional.)

5. Pour sauce into a blender and purée until smooth. Stir in red pepper pulp, mint, and lime juice to taste. Keep warm until ready to serve.

6. Sprinkle swordfish steaks with salt. Heat oil in a large sauté pan over high heat. When hot, add swordfish and sauté for 3 or 4 minutes, or until a crust has formed. Lower heat to medium. Turn swordfish and sauté until opaque. Do not overcook.

7. Place a swordfish steak off center on each of four hot service plates. Arrange *Broccoli-Pickled Eggplant Stir-Fry* on the other side of the plate.

8. Ladle the toasted rice sauce between the fish and the vegetables.

9. Sprinkle rice sauce and surrounding plate surface with pulverized rice. Sprinkle vegetables with julienned red pepper. Serve immediately.

FOR ONE SERVING (With rice sauce and vegetables): 420 Calories; 10.2 grams Fat (1.9 Saturated); 40 mg Cholesterol.

FILLET OF SOLE PICASSO

Treasure the minimal production time of this dish graced with kiwi, orange, and strawberries from Cafe L'Europe in Sarasota, Florida.

4 Servings
Preparation Time: 10 minutes
Cooking Time: 10 minutes

HEALTH TIP: *Canola oil is a monounsaturated oil with a very high (440-degree) "smoking point," making it excellent for quick sautéing. It is a light-colored, flavorless oil that doesn't interfere with the taste of delicate ingredients like the fruit in this recipe.*

4 6-oz. fillets of lemon
  sole
1½ tbsp. rice flour or
  plain flour
1 tbsp. white pepper
4 tbsp. canola oil
½ cup lemon juice
¼ cup white wine

2 large oranges, peeled
  and sliced
4 kiwi, peeled and sliced
4 strawberries, cut in half
2 tbsp. melted reduced-
  calorie margarine
  (optional)

1. Lightly dust the sole with the flour and pepper. In a hot skillet, heat oil, then brown the sole on both sides until golden brown. Just before removing sole from skillet, add the lemon juice and wine.

2. Place sole in a baking dish and top with wine sauce. Arrange sliced fruit on top. Place under broiler to warm the fruit. Drizzle melted margarine over fruit, if desired. Serve with steamed vegetables.

ONE SERVING: 389 Calories; 17.1 grams Fat (2.9 Saturated); 79 mg Cholesterol.

GRILLED TUNA ON ROASTED VEGETABLES WITH PINEAPPLE-SOY VINAIGRETTE

Jeff Tunks' way of oven roasting vegetables produces a robust, aromatic accompaniment to charcoal grilled tuna—perfect for a low-sodium diet. Jeff Tunks is the chef at the River Club in Washington, D.C., an Art Deco club where you may dance to forties' music and dine on nineties' cuisine.

4 Servings
Preparation Time: 20 minutes
Cooking Time: 30 minutes

HEALTH TIP: The vegetables in this dish are chock full of unrefined fiber which takes time to digest; thereby maintaining blood sugar on an even keel and preventing hunger pangs.

1½ lb. yellowfin tuna loin
1 tbsp. olive oil
1 zucchini, diced
1 yellow squash, diced
1 large tomato, diced
½ cup quartered shitake
  mushrooms
1 14-oz. can artichoke
  hearts, rinsed,
  drained, and
  quartered
1 bulb fresh fennel,
  coarsely chopped
1 large carrot, sliced
1½ tbsp. olive oil
½ cup chopped fresh
  basil leaves

1 tbsp. sodium-reduced
  soy sauce
1 tbsp. salad oil
1 tbsp. rice wine vinegar
1 tbsp. sesame oil
1 tsp. minced fresh ginger
½ tbsp. toasted sesame
  seeds
4 scallions, slivered
½ cup diced fresh
  pineapple or one
  8-oz. can, drained and
  diced
fresh basil leaves for
  garnish

1. Preheat oven to 350 degrees. Preheat grill. Cut tuna into four steaks. Coat with 1 tablespoon olive oil.

2. Place zucchini, squash, tomato, mushrooms, artichoke hearts, fennel, and carrot in a shallow roasting pan. Toss with remaining 1½ tablespoons olive oil and the basil leaves. Roast at 350 degrees until tender, 20 to 30 minutes.

3. In a food processor, combine soy sauce, salad oil, vinegar, sesame oil, ginger, sesame seeds, and scallions. Process briefly, then stir in pineapple.

4. Grill tuna until just tender, about 5 minutes on each side. Do not overcook. Arrange tuna steaks on top of roasted vegetables on serving plates. Pour vinaigrette over all. Garnish with fresh basil leaves and serve immediately.

ONE SERVING: 453 Calories; 22.2 grams Fat (3.2 Saturated); 30 mg Cholesterol.

BAKED GULF FISH WITH HORSERADISH CRUST

Name your *poisson*—any mild fillet baked with this crisp coating and finished with the tomato leek sauce will be fantastic. Commander's Palace chef, Jamie Shannon, cooks in an area of our country where seafood is king—New Orleans, Louisiana.

4 Servings
Preparation Time: 15 minutes
Cooking Time: 25 minutes

5 oz. prepared
    horseradish
½ cup plain bread
    crumbs
2 tbsp. softened butter
1 tbsp. olive oil
3 tbsp. finely chopped
    leek (white part only)
2 tsp. minced garlic
1 cup chopped tomato
    (peeled and seeded)
1¼ cups white wine
1 cup strong chicken
    stock
1 tsp. finely chopped
    fresh thyme

1 tsp. finely chopped
    fresh oregano
1 tsp. finely chopped
    fresh basil
⅛ tsp. salt
3 tsp. cornstarch
¼ tsp. freshly ground
    black pepper
4 7-oz. fillets of white fish
    (grouper, amberjack,
    cusk, etc.)
salt and white pepper
1 tbsp. chopped parsley
    for garnish

1. Preheat oven to 400 degrees.

2. In a bowl, combine horseradish, bread crumbs, and butter. Set aside.

3. In a large sauté pan over medium-high heat, heat olive oil; then add leeks, garlic, tomatoes, 1 cup white wine, stock, thyme, oregano, basil, and salt. Cook until the mixture is reduced by half, about 10 minutes.

4. In a small bowl, combine cornstarch and remaining ¼ cup white wine. Add to sauté pan and cook, stirring, for five minutes. Add black pepper and keep sauce warm.

HINT: You may wish to run the fish under the broiler at the end of the baking time to produce a golden brown crust.

5. Season fish with salt and white pepper. Divide horseradish mixture and coat each fillet, covering the tops well. Place fish in a greased 9 x 12 baking dish and bake at 400 degrees for 10 to 15 minutes. Remove from oven, then ladle ¼ sauce on each of four plates. Top with baked fish and garnish with ¼ tablespoon of parsley.

ONE SERVING: 349 Calories; 10.8 grams Fat (3.7 Saturated); 39 mg Cholesterol.

"See those clouds; how they hang! That's the greatest thing I have seen today. I thought, I might go a-fishing. That's the true industry for poets. It's the only trade I have learned. Come, let's along!"

Henry David Thoreau

HEALTH TIP: This recipe is ideal for a very low-fat diet. It is recommended that we limit daily fat intake to thirty percent of total caloric intake. Each gram of fat contains nine calories, while there are only four calories per gram of protein or carbohydrate.

MAHIMAHI OPORTO

By adding a bit more cayenne and chili peppers, you can adjust the thermostat on this dish from Cafe L'Europe. If mahimahi isn't in the seafood case, most any fish will be fine—especially one just off your hook!

4 Servings
Preparation Time: 10 minutes
Cooking Time: 15 minutes

4 tbsp. fresh lime juice	2 tbsp. minced mild green
⅛ tsp. cayenne pepper	chile pepper
1¼ lb. mahimahi	1 large tomato, chopped
cooking oil spray	2 tbsp. white wine
1 onion, sliced	2 tsp. lemon juice
1 bell pepper (green, yellow, or red), chopped	

1. Sprinkle lime juice and cayenne pepper on fish.

2. Spray a skillet with cooking oil and sauté onion, bell pepper, and chili pepper for 2 minutes. Add fish to skillet and cover with tomato, spooning the onion-pepper mixture over fish also. Add wine and lemon juice. Simmer, turning fish once, until fish is done, about 8 minutes.

ONE SERVING: 260 Calories; 2 grams Fat; 85 mg Cholesterol.

BROILED FILLET OF
PACIFIC HALIBUT WITH
CILANTRO-ARTICHOKE RELISH

First quality ingredients shine in this savory dish from the dining room of the elegant Ritz Carlton hotel in Chicago, where Pascal Vignau is the chef.

4 Servings
Preparation and Cooking Time: 1 hour

4 5-oz. Pacific halibut
    fillets, ¼ inch thick
salt and pepper to taste
4 tbsp. virgin olive oil
2 raw artichoke bottoms,
    cleaned and minced
½ cup lemon juice
1 red bell pepper, roasted,
    peeled, and julienned

1 bunch fresh cilantro,
    cleaned and finely
    chopped
20 green artichoke leaves,
    cooked until tender
    in boiling water (for
    garnish)

IN A HURRY?: To simplify preparation, buy deli-roasted red peppers, use canned or frozen artichoke bottoms, and garnish with cilantro leaves.

VARIATION: Any thin, white fish can be substituted for the Pacific halibut.

1. Preheat oven to 400 degrees.

2. Season the halibut with salt and pepper. Pour 2 tablespoons olive oil into a flat roasting pan; place halibut on top and bake at 400 degrees for 3 minutes. Remove from oven.

3. In a heavy skillet over medium-low heat, heat the remaining 2 tablespoons of olive oil; then sauté minced artichokes for about 5 minutes. Add lemon juice, roasted red pepper, and cilantro. Remove from heat.

4. Just before serving, return halibut to 400-degree oven for 3 minutes. Due to thinness of fillets, it is not necessary to turn fish.

5. To serve, remove artichokes from skillet with a slotted spoon and place on a serving plate. Arrange halibut fillets on top of minced artichokes; then pour juice from skillet over fillets. Decorate with artichoke leaves.

ONE SERVING: 310 Calories; 16 grams Fat (2.4 Saturated); 0 mg Cholesterol.

VARIATION: *Another time, try toasting slices of French baguette, coat with a light brush of butter and a sprinkle of Creole Seasoning. Top with crabmeat mixture.*

BON TON CAFE'S CRABMEAT IMPERIAL

The Bon Ton Cafe is widely recognized as the first restaurant in New Orleans to serve Cajun cooking. All of the Cajun dishes are prepared from family recipes that originated along the bayous deep in Cajun territory. Chef Wayne Pierce says, "Crabmeat Imperial is not only light in the dietary sense, but also in the meaning interpreted in tropical climates, such as New Orleans, where temperatures and humidity dictate eating habits during the summer months."

4 Servings
Preparation Time: 15 minutes
Cooking Time: 6 to 8 minutes

4 tbsp. margarine
¾ cup chopped green onions
½ cup thinly sliced mushrooms
20 oz. fresh lump crabmeat
½ cup chopped pimentos

¾ cup sherry
salt and freshly ground pepper to taste
4 slices bread, toasted and quartered
⅓ cup finely chopped parsley

1. In a large skillet over low heat, melt 1 tablespoon of margarine. Add green onions and cook until soft; then add mushrooms and cook until mushrooms are tender.

2. In a small bowl, combine crabmeat, pimentos, and sherry.

3. Cut the remaining 3 tablespoons margarine into thin slices. Add to skillet along with the crabmeat mixture. Gently mix together until heated through. Season to taste with salt and pepper.

4. On each serving plate, arrange 4 crispy toast points. Serve crab over toast, sprinkled with chopped parsley.

ONE SERVING: 303 Calories; 14.2 grams Fat (2.3 Saturated); 112 mg Cholesterol.

DRY-FRIED SHRIMP WITH ROASTED SHALLOTS

Don't skimp on the marinating time for this popular dish from Hamersley's Bistro in Boston. The garlicky shrimp are cooked in the shell, making them extra moist and succulent. In *Food and Wine* magazine, the food critic for *Boston Magazine*, Rene Becker says, "If I judged a restaurant by how often I like to eat there, Hamersley's would be my hands-down favorite."

4 Servings
Preparation and Cooking Time: 35 minutes
Marinate: 3 to 4 hours
Roasting Time: 1½ hours

1 tbsp. plus 4 tsp. olive
  oil
1 tbsp. fresh lemon juice
½ lemon, sliced
3 cloves garlic, minced
1 tsp. minced plus 20
  unpeeled whole
  shallots
1 tsp. chopped fresh
  thyme (or ½ tsp.
  dried)
pinch fennel seeds
pinch crushed red pepper
  flakes

1 lb. large shrimp,
  unpeeled
1 1½-lb. celery root,
  peeled and cut into
  ½-inch cubes
1 bunch (about 1 lb.)
  kale, in bite-sized
  pieces
¼ cup sherry vinegar or
  balsamic vinegar
½ tsp. chopped fresh
  sage (or pinch dried)
salt and freshly ground
  pepper to taste

1. In a non-aluminum dish, combine 1 tablespoon olive oil, lemon juice, lemon slices, 1 minced garlic clove, 1 teaspoon minced shallots, thyme, fennel, and red pepper. Add shrimp and toss to coat. Cover and refrigerate for 3 to 4 hours.

2. Preheat oven to 325 degrees. In a small roasting pan, toss unpeeled shallots with 1 teaspoon olive oil. Cover and bake for 1 to 1¼ hours, or until they are very tender, shaking the pan occasionally. Let cool, slip off the skins, and set aside.

NOTE: Rinse kale very well, remove the stalks, and tear into bite-sized pieces. When purchasing kale, look for crisp, dark green or purple leaves. Store in the refrigerator and use within 2 or 3 days.

HEALTH TIP: Kale is one of the most nutritious vegetables available to us. A member of the cancer-preventing cabbage family, it rates high in potassium and calcium, and is a good source of protein and iron. All of this nourishment measures in at only forty-three calories per cup of cooked kale.

3. Blanch celery root in a large pot of boiling, salted water for 4 to 5 minutes, or until crisp and tender. Drain and refresh with cold water.

4. In a large, non-stick skillet, heat 2 teaspoons olive oil over medium heat. Add celery root and remaining 2 cloves minced garlic and sauté for 1 to 2 minutes, or until the garlic has softened. Add shallots, kale, vinegar, and sage; then sauté for 5 to 6 minutes, or until the kale has wilted. Season with salt and pepper. Set aside in a covered bowl and keep warm.

5. Wash and dry the skillet; then heat the remaining teaspoon olive oil over high heat until hot, but not smoking. Remove shrimp from marinade (discard marinade) and sauté for 2 to 3 minutes, or just until pink.

6. Divide vegetables among 4 plates and place the shrimp around the vegetables. Serve immediately.

ONE SERVING: 245 Calories; 8 grams Fat; 173 mg Cholesterol.

HEALTH TIP: Serve with rice and steamed broccoli to fortify the meal with additional calcium, fiber, and vitamin A.

TUNA DECATUR

A Cajun crab-vegetable sauce from The Court of Two Sisters creates palate-pleasing excitement when paired with any grilled fish. Peter Ferroe wears the toque at The Court of Two Sisters in the heart of the French Quarter. This restaurant-landmark is especially well known for the daily Plantation Jazz Brunch Buffet that typifies the sensuousness of all that is New Orleans.

8 Servings
Preparation Time: 15 minutes
Cooking Time: 20 minutes

8 6-oz. fresh tuna steaks,
 ¾-inch thick
1 lb. fresh lump crabmeat
1 lb. shrimp, cooked,
 peeled, and deveined
¼ cup finely chopped
 celery
¼ cup finely chopped
 white onion
¼ cup finely chopped red
 bell pepper
¼ cup tomatoes, skinned,
 seeded, and diced
¼ cup sliced mushrooms
2 tbsp. olive oil
2 drops hot red pepper
 sauce
1 tbsp. lemon juice
¼ cup red wine vinegar
1 tsp. coarse black
 pepper
salt to taste

1. Preheat grill.

2. Rinse tuna under cold water, then pat dry. Grill to desired doneness.

3. In a large skillet, combine the remaining ingredients. Bring to a strong simmer and cook for about 2 minutes. Serve about ½ cup sauce over each tuna steak.

ONE SERVING: 477 Calories; 13.5 grams Fat (2.3 Saturated); 195 mg Cholesterol.

BAKED EGGPLANT WITH SEAFOOD

Take a spicy crab cake and bake it on top of an eggplant slice; then serve it up with an array of colorful vegetables. This is quite a crowd pleaser from Commander's Palace, which was one of *Money* magazine's "Top Three Restaurants in New Orleans."

4 Servings
Preparation Time: 20 minutes
Cooking Time: 50 minutes

MAKE AHEAD: May be prepared in advance through Step Three. Refrigerate, then bring to room temperature before continuing.

3 cups diced eggplant
5 cups water
1 tbsp. salt
2 tbsp. olive oil
1 cup finely chopped
   yellow onion
2 tbsp. finely chopped red
   pepper
2 tbsp. finely chopped
   green pepper
2 tbsp. finely chopped
   celery
1 tbsp. chopped garlic
2 tbsp. julienned basil
   leaves
1 tbsp. finely chopped
   thyme
1 cup coarsely chopped
   shrimp

½ cup coarsely chopped
   fish
5 oz. white wine
1½ cup diced French
   bread
2 tsp. parmesan cheese
½ cup fresh lump
   crabmeat
1 medium eggplant,
   sliced lengthwise into
   four ¾-inch slices
2 cups thinly sliced
   purple cabbage
salt and pepper
2 tbsp. extra virgin olive
   oil
1 large tomato, cut into
   8 wedges
1 large lemon, cut into
   8 wedges

1. Preheat oven to 350 degrees.

2. In a saucepan, place diced eggplant into water, add salt, and bring to a boil. Cook for about 15 minutes, or until tender. Drain.

3. In an ovenproof sauté pan, heat 1 tablespoon olive oil. Add onion, peppers, celery, garlic, basil, and thyme. Sauté for about 5 minutes. Add cooked diced eggplant, shrimp, fish, and white wine; then cook until seafood is done, about 2 minutes. Add bread and parmesan cheese.

4. Place in a 350-degree oven for 5 minutes. Remove from oven and fold in crabmeat.

5. Place ¾ cup of the baked mixture on each slice of fresh eggplant. Place on baking sheet in a 350-degree oven, and bake for 10 minutes.

6. In a sauté pan, heat 1 tablespoon olive oil. Add purple cabbage and sauté until limp. Season with salt and pepper.

7. To serve, divide the cabbage onto four plates, spreading it out to cover the bottom of each plate. Place the baked eggplant in the center and drizzle ½ tablespoon extra virgin olive oil over eggplant. Garnish each plate with 2 wedges of tomato and 2 wedges of lemon.

ONE SERVING: 370 Calories; 15.2 grams Fat (2.5 Saturated); 158 mg Cholesterol.

GRILLED LOBSTER AND SCALLOP KEBOBS

At The Treetop House in Berkley, West Virginia, Chef Robert Siegworth serves this delectable seafood treat with his *Pecan Brown Rice*.

6 Servings
Marinate: 5 hours
Cooking Time: 10 to 12 minutes

½ cup white wine
¼ cup fresh lemon juice
3 large cloves garlic, minced
1 tbsp. chopped fresh dill
1 tsp. freshly ground black pepper
2 tbsp. margarine, melted

1 lb. sea scallops, in 1-oz. pieces
1 lb. lobster tail meat, in 1-oz. pieces
cooking oil spray
1 recipe Pecan Brown Rice (see index for recipe)

1. Preheat grill.

2. In a shallow dish, combine wine, lemon juice, garlic, dill, pepper, and margarine. Add scallops and lobster, turning to coat. Marinate for 5 hours.

3. Remove seafood, reserving marinade. Divide seafood between 4 skewers. Brush with marinade. Coat grill with cooking oil spray. Grill kebobs for 10 to 12 minutes, turning and basting frequently with marinade, until meat turns white. Serve with *Pecan Brown Rice*.

ONE SERVING (With ½ cup rice): 322 Calories; 12.8 grams Fat (2.8 Saturated); 82 mg Cholesterol.

VARIATION: Thick fillets of fish, such as shark or swordfish (and especially monkfish with its lobster-like flavor), can be cubed, marinated for one hour, and used for the kabobs instead of lobster and scallops.

HINT: If fresh dill is not available, substitute dried but, as in any recipe, you will need less. The general rule is to use three times more of a fresh herb than dried.

SHRIMP CREOLE

Nothing says "Louisiana cooking" like Shrimp Creole. This version, heavy on flavor and light on calories, is from Lafitte's Landing in Donaldsonville.

4 Servings
Preparation Time: 25 minutes
Cooking Time: 15 minutes

4 tsp. vegetable oil	2 tsp. Worcestershire
1 cup sliced onion	sauce
¼ cup sliced celery	salt and cayenne pepper
¼ cup chopped red or	to taste
green bell peppers	½ tsp. dried oregano
1 tsp. chopped garlic	1 bay leaf
3 cups canned whole	1 lb. (21 to 25 count)
tomatoes, drained	shrimp, peeled and
and chopped (reserve	deveined
liquid)	¼ cup chopped parsley
2 tsp. tomato paste	2 cups cooked long-grain
	rice

1. In a large saucepan, heat oil over medium-high heat. Add onion, celery, pepper, and garlic. Sauté until vegetables are tender; then stir in reserved tomato liquid, tomatoes, tomato paste, Worcestershire sauce, salt, cayenne pepper, oregano, and bay leaf. Bring to a boil. Stir in shrimp and 2 tablespoons parsley. Continue cooking just until shrimp turns pink. Remove bay leaf.

2. Arrange rice on serving platter and top with shrimp mixture. Garnish with remaining 2 tablespoons of parsley.

ONE SERVING (With ½ cup rice): 322 Calories; 7.4 grams Fat (1.2 Saturated); 198 mg Cholesterol.

HEALTH TIP: When choosing peppers, remember that red peppers contain six times more vitamin A than green peppers.

IN A HURRY? When just a small amount of tomato paste is required, tubes of tomato paste are very handy. Just squeeze out a tablespoon or two, and store the tube in the refrigerator for the next time. They can be purchased in the canned tomato section of most supermarkets.

SEA SCALLOP SAUTE
WITH BLACK BEAN AND
CHIPOTLE STEW

Janos Wilder gives scallops a Southwestern zing by combining them with hot peppers and plenty of garlic and lime. Janos Wilder, the chef and owner of Janos in Tucson, Arizona, is one of James Beard's "Rising Stars in American Cuisine."

4 Servings
Preparation and Cooking Time: 20 minutes

olive oil
2 cups slivered green
    onions
1 cup fresh corn kernels
½ cup roasted, peeled,
    seeded, and diced
    Anaheim chilies
2 tbsp. chopped garlic
2 cups dry white wine
2 cups fish stock (or
    bottled clam juice)
2 cups diced fresh
    tomatoes

2 cups cooked black
    beans
1 oz. finely chopped
    chipotle peppers (or
    jalapenos)
1½ lb. sea scallops, well
    rinsed and cleaned
1 cup fresh cilantro
    leaves
4 oz. lime juice
salt and pepper to taste

1. Coat a large skillet with olive oil and briefly sauté green onions, corn, Anaheim chilies, and garlic. Add wine and fish stock; then simmer for about 2 minutes. Add scallops and cook just until they turn white.

2. Add tomatoes, beans, and chipotle peppers; then combine thoroughly. Add cilantro and lime juice, then salt and pepper to taste. Serve in bowls.

ONE SERVING: 290 Calories; 3.8 grams Fat (0.7 Saturated); 27 mg Cholesterol.

NOTE: Chipotle peppers are mature (red) jalapenos which have been smoked, then canned. They can be found in Mexican specialty markets. In this recipe, chopped fresh jalapenos can be used in their place.

IN A HURRY? The preparation time listed is based on using prepared chipotle, roasted Anaheim chilies, black beans, and fish stock.

SWEET CORN SAUCE FOR SEAFOOD

Don Pintabona, chef at the Tribeca grill in New York City says, "This bright yellow sauce is delicious with red snap-per, orange roughy, or shrimp."

Makes about 1½ cups
Preparation Time: 10 minutes
Cooking Time: 35 minutes

4 ears corn
2 cups chicken stock or canned low-salt broth
¼ cup diced tomatoes
¼ cup finely diced green bell pepper

¼ cup finely diced yellow bell pepper
2 tbsp. chopped green onion

1. Cut corn kernels from cob. Cut each corn cob into 4 pieces. Place corn cobs in a large saucepan, add stock, and bring to a boil. Cook over medium heat until liquid is re-duced to 1 cup, about 10 minutes.

2. Strain into another large saucepan, pressing on cobs with the back of a spoon. Add all but ¼ cup of the corn ker-nels to stock mixture and cook over medium-high heat for 15 minutes. Allow to cool slightly.

3. In a processor, purée stock mixture. Strain through a sieve set over a bowl, pressing on solids with the back of a spoon.

4. In a heavy, medium saucepan, bring purée to a simmer. Add reserved ¼ cup corn kernels, tomatoes, bell peppers, and onions. Stir to heat through.

ONE SERVING (¼ cup): 66 Calories; 1.2 grams Fat; 0 mg Cholesterol.

SWORDFISH IN
MUSTARD SEED CRUST

This specialty of Van Dyke Place in Detroit, Michigan is ready to eat in under 30 minutes—and just wait 'til you taste what a mustard coating does for swordfish!

4 Servings
Preparation Time: 10 minutes
Cooking Time: 6-8 minutes

4 6-oz. swordfish steaks   **2 tbsp. mustard seed**
black pepper   **2 tbsp. olive oil**
4 tbsp. grainy mustard

1. Preheat broiler.

2. Season swordfish with black pepper thoroughly. Coat top side of fish with a mixture of mustard, mustard seed, and olive oil.

3. Broil about 4 inches from heat for 6 to 8 minutes. Do not turn fish. Mustard coating should be crisp, while fish is still moist, but cooked thoroughly.

ONE SERVING: 248 Calories; 12.6 grams Fat (2.0 Saturated); 94 mg Cholesterol.

NICE WITH: Lemon wedges, steamed redskin potatoes topped with chopped black olives, and pan-warmed cherry tomatoes.

HINT: When oven broiling skinless fish like the swordfish in this recipe, preheat the broiler for five to eight minutes. Place fish fillets or steaks on the broiler pan and cook for about seven to eight minutes without turning. For fish fillets with a skin (like snapper), place skin side up, broil for about four minutes, then turn the fish over and peel the skin off. Continue broiling until cooked.

Poultry

Poultry

Chicken Breasts with Morels

Grilled Chicken with Tomato-Pepper Salsa, Lemon-Caper
Rice, and Asparagus

Lucy Chu's Poached Chicken

Chicken with Raspberry Vinegar

Stonehill Chicken

Coq au Riesling

Chilled Chicken with Spicy Sauce

Breast of Chicken Poached with Vegetables and Fine Herbs

Chicken with Mustard-Yogurt Sauce

Lemon Pepper Chicken

Cuban Chicken Mojo

Enchiladas Verdes

Le Supreme de Poulet a la Provençale

Grilled Chicken with Salad and Fresh Herbs

Breast of Duck with Raspberry-Black Bean Gastrique

Cornish Game Hen with Orange Apricot Sauce

Chicken Ajillo Iberian

Breast of Pheasant with Celery Root and
Cranberry-Pepper Sauce

Cast Iron Seared and Roasted Pheasant

Grilled Chicken with Honey, Lime, and Garlic Glaze

CHICKEN BREASTS WITH MORELS

At l'Auberge in Dayton, Ohio, Chef Dieter Krug understands that often the best cooking is the result of minimal processing—and he has the international awards to prove it. In this recipe, tender chicken is blessed with a simple concentrate of rich stock, morels, and wine.

4 Servings
Preparation Time: 10 minutes
Cooking Time: 20 minutes

4 6-oz. boneless chicken breasts	1 tsp. butter
16 fresh morel mushrooms	1 tbsp. vegetable oil
salt and white pepper	1 shallot, diced
	2 tbsp. dry white wine
	⅔ cup rich veal stock

1. Remove the skin, fat, and tendons from the chicken breasts. Split the morels lengthwise, wash them quickly with a little vinegar and cold water, then dry them well.

2. Season the chicken with salt and white pepper to taste. In a large skillet, heat the butter and oil over medium-high heat until hot. Add the chicken and sauté until golden brown and cooked through. Remove chicken and keep warm.

3. Wipe skillet with paper towel to remove grease, then add the shallots, morels, and white wine. Cook over medium heat until syrupy. Add the veal stock and reduce by half. Season to taste with salt and pepper.

4. Place chicken on serving plate, top with morel sauce, and serve.

ONE SERVING: 281 Calories; 10.0 grams Fat (2.7 Saturated); 123 mg Cholesterol.

GRILLED CHICKEN WITH TOMATO-PEPPER SALSA, LEMON-CAPER RICE, AND ASPARAGUS

Multiple flavors explode in this colorful dish from Commander's Palace. Jamie Shannon, chef at the famous restaurant in New Orleans, prepared the chicken and salsa for their daily featured light meal. "It has been a big hit!" he reported.

4 Servings
Preparation Time: 30 minutes

½ cup diced ripe
   tomatoes, seeded
¼ cup diced green pepper
¼ cup diced yellow
   pepper
10 grinds black pepper
1 tsp. tequila
1 tsp. plus 1 tbsp. olive
   oil
1 tsp. finely chopped
   cilantro

1 cup long-grain rice
5½ cups water
2 tsp. salt
½ tsp. white pepper
juice of 2 lemons
2 tbsp. capers
16 thin asparagus spears
4 boneless, skinless
   chicken breasts
   (about 2 lb.)

1. Prepare salsa by combining tomatoes, peppers, black pepper, tequila, 1 teaspoon of olive oil, and cilantro. Refrigerate.

2. In a small saucepan, combine rice with 1½ cups water, 1 teaspoon salt, and pepper. Bring to a boil, reduce heat, and cover. Simmer for 15 minutes, then add lemon juice and capers. Keep warm.

3. Boil 4 cups water, then add 1 teaspoon salt and asparagus. Cook until desired tenderness.

4. Rub chicken with remaining tablespoon of olive oil and cook until done on a grill or in a hot sauté pan, about 5 minutes on each side.

5. To serve, place ½ cup rice in center of each plate. Place chicken breast on top, and garnish with 4 asparagus spears and ¼ cup salsa.

ONE SERVING (With rice and salsa): 463 Calories; 11.2 grams Fat (2.4 Saturated); 143 mg Cholesterol.

NOTE: For chicken breasts, boil over high heat for only eight minutes and let stand in the broth for just one hour.

HEALTH TIP: A switch to lighter, simpler cooking begs the use of a versatile, nutritious ingredient like poached chicken breasts. A 3.5-ounce serving of cooked (skinless) white meat of chicken supplies: 173 calories; 1.3 grams of saturated fat; 85 milligrams of cholesterol; and 30 grams of protein.

LUCY CHU'S POACHED CHICKEN

Mrs. Chu, who teaches this method at her cooking school in Columbus, Ohio, says, "Cooking with low heat draws the juices out; this is fine for sauces, but not for meat. To get the best, juiciest poached chicken ever, boil it, completely covered with liquid, over a very hot flame."

8 Servings
Cooking Time: 12 minutes
Soaking Time: 2 hours

1 2-lb. cut-up chicken (or chicken breasts)

3 qt. water or chicken stock
salt and pepper

1. In a large, heavy pot, bring the water or stock to a rolling boil. Submerge the chicken pieces completely, and boil over high heat for 12 minutes, keeping the lid on.

2. Remove from heat. Leave the chicken in the broth for 2 hours; then remove from bones, add salt and pepper, and serve or chill for later use.

ONE SERVING (4 oz.): 216.8 Calories; 8.4 g Fat (2.2 Saturated); 101 mg Cholesterol.

CHICKEN WITH RASPBERRY VINEGAR

Highly regarded chef, Michael Foley, is cooking up a low-calorie storm at Printer's Row in Chicago. This is his innovative way of cooking moist, flavorful chicken.

6 Servings
Preparation and Cooking Time: 50 minutes

2 tbsp. raspberry vinegar
1 qt. chicken stock
1 tsp. tomato paste
2 cloves garlic, minced
¼ cup tomato, finely
   chopped
6 chicken legs
6 chicken thighs
6 6-oz. boneless chicken
   breasts

3 tsp. unsalted butter,
   cold
18 fresh tarragon leaves
6 medium potatoes
1 tsp. whole grain
   mustard
1 tbsp. finely chopped
   fresh chives
1 tbsp. thinly sliced fresh
   basil

1. Preheat oven to 350 degrees.

2. In a large saucepan, combine raspberry vinegar, chicken stock, tomato paste, garlic, and half of the chopped tomato. Bring to a boil. Add chicken legs and thighs, loosely cover, and simmer for about 20 minutes. (To check for doneness, pierce with a fork; juices should run clear.)

3. Prepare chicken breasts while legs and thighs are cooking. Holding knife parallel to working surface, slit each breast 1 inch deep, making a small pocket. Place ½ teaspoon butter and 3 tarragon leaves in each pocket. Place each breast in a 6 x 6 piece of aluminum foil and wrap securely.

4. Remove legs and thighs from saucepan and place in another pan with a cover. Return stock mixture to boiling. Drop wrapped breasts into stock, loosely cover, and simmer for about 12 minutes. Remove packets from stock and transfer (still wrapped) to pan with legs and thighs.

HEALTH TIP: Chef Foley prefers to use free-range chickens. These are grain-fed birds that have been allowed to roam the barnyard, scratching and developing naturally, as their ancestors did. One taste and you will remember how good chicken can be! Call your health food store to find out whether there is a breeder who supplies free-range chicken in your area.

5. Prepare potatoes while chicken breasts are cooking. Cut each potato into ½-inch slices and arrange in a single layer in a shallow non-stick pan. Roast potatoes in preheated oven for 15 to 20 minutes.

6. To finish sauce, heat stock mixture over high heat for about 15 minutes to reduce to 1½ to 2 cups liquid. Add the chopped tomato and any liquid accumulated in covered pan. Stir in mustard, and cook over low heat for 5 minutes.

7. On each serving plate, place one breast, one leg, one thigh and a few roasted potato slices. Ladle sauce over all and sprinkle with chives and basil.

ONE SERVING: 451 Calories; 10.7 grams Fat (3.0 Saturated); 149 mg Cholesterol.

STONEHILL CHICKEN

Executive Chef Philip McGrath impresses members of The Doubles Club in New York City with upscale menu choices like this crispy chicken with a Mediterranean accent.

4 Servings
Preparation Time: 20 minutes
Cooking Time: 25 minutes

4 6-oz. boneless, skinless
  chicken breasts
salt and freshly ground
  pepper to taste
cornmeal
2 tbsp. olive oil
2 medium artichoke
  bottoms, cut into
  wedges
12 medium shitake
  mushrooms,
  stemmed, then cut
  into wedges
2 cloves garlic, minced

2 medium shallots,
  minced
1 tsp. chopped Italian
  parsley
1 tsp. chopped fresh
  rosemary
1 tsp. chopped chives
4 tbsp. balsamic vinegar
1 cup chicken stock
½ cup cooked chick peas
  (garbanzo beans)
4 plum tomatoes, peeled,
  seeded, and diced

1. Season the chicken with salt and pepper, then dredge lightly in cornmeal.

2. In a 10-inch skillet, heat the oil until hot, but not smoking. Sauté the chicken until golden brown on both sides and juices run clear when pierced with a knife, about 8 minutes. Remove chicken from pan, blot with paper towels, and keep warm.

3. Add artichoke and mushrooms to skillet. Sauté until artichokes are brown and mushrooms are tender. Add garlic and shallots. Cook for one minute.

4. In a small bowl, combine parsley, rosemary, and chives. Add ¾ of the herb mixture to the skillet and combine gently.

5. Add vinegar and cook until reduced by half. Add chicken stock and chick-peas; then reduce by half again. Add tomatoes and check seasoning. Add salt or pepper if desired.

6. Spoon the vegetable and sauce mixture onto each serving plate. Place a chicken breast on top and sprinkle with the remaining herb mixture.

ONE SERVING: 302 Calories; 11.16 grams Fat (2.1 Saturated); 95 mg Cholesterol.

COQ AU RIESLING

The aroma wafting from the kitchen as you put together this updated version of coq au vin is irresistible. This recipe is from Chef Debra Ponzek, who was named "Woman Chef of the Year" for the talents she displays at her New York City restaurant, Montrachet.

6 Servings
Preparation Time: 25 minutes
Marinate: 12 hours
Cooking Time: 40 minutes

NICE WITH: Chef Ponzek serves this with spatzle, tiny German egg noodles made with a special cutter or by pressing dough through a colander. Plain noodles cooked in chicken broth would be very good as well—and much quicker!

HINT: No need to peel the onions; the skins slip off easily after parboiling.

4 Cornish hens, about
1¼ lb. each
salt and pepper
1¼ cup coarsely chopped
shallots
4 sprigs fresh thyme
1 cup Riesling wine
1 tbsp. olive oil
16 pearl onions, blanched
for 10 minutes
4 carrots, cut into ½-inch
cubes, blanched for
10 minutes
3 turnips, cut into ½-inch
cubes, boiled for 4 to
5 minutes
10 large white
mushrooms, cut into
½-inch cubes
6 thick slices bacon,
diced, sautéed, and
drained
1¼ cup chicken broth
1½ tbsp. chopped fresh
tarragon

1. Cut each hen into 6 serving pieces and season with salt and pepper. Place in a bowl with shallots and thyme and mix well. Add the wine, cover, and marinate for 12 hours.

2. Remove the pieces of hen, reserving marinade. In a large skillet over medium heat, heat the olive oil; then brown hen pieces, skin side down, for about 5 minutes. Add the onions, carrots, turnips, mushrooms, and bacon. Cook, stirring, for about 3 minutes. Cover and cook over low heat for 8 to 10 minutes.

3. Remove the hen pieces and keep warm. Add the reserved marinade and chicken broth to the skillet. Increase heat to medium, and cook until reduced to about one cup. Add the hen pieces and the tarragon. Bring to a boil, divide into 6 portions of 4 pieces of hen topped with vegetables and sauce, and serve immediately.

ONE SERVING: 499 Calories; 27.7 grams Fat (8.0 Saturated); 155 mg Cholesterol.

CHILLED CHICKEN WITH SPICY SAUCE

MAKE AHEAD: *If made ahead through Step Three, last-minute kitchen time will be minimal.*

Lucy Chu, a native of Shanghai, China, teaches cooking on cruise ships such as the *Queen Elizabeth II*, the *SS Oceanic*, and the *Golden Odyssey*. She suggests serving the spiced chicken over steamed broccoli florets as a delicious alternative to the lettuce.

HEALTH TIP: *When you remove the fatty skin from chicken, each three-ounce serving loses forty calories.*

4 Servings
Preparation Time and Cooking Time: 2½ hours

1 lb. boneless, skinless chicken breast	½ tsp. Szechwan peppercorns, crushed
2 quarts water or chicken stock	¼ tsp. crushed red pepper
3 tbsp. vegetable oil	4 tbsp. soy sauce
½ cup chopped scallions	2 tbsp. honey
1 tsp. minced ginger	½ tsp. salt (optional)
1 tsp. minced garlic	lettuce leaves

1. In a heavy pot, bring the water or stock to a rolling boil. Submerge chicken breasts completely and boil over high heat for 8 minutes, keeping the lid on. Remove from heat, and leave the chicken in the broth for one hour. After poaching, chill chicken for at least one hour.

2. In a skillet over low heat, heat the oil; then add the scallions, ginger, garlic, peppercorns, and crushed red pepper. Cook for one minute, then turn off heat.

3. In a small bowl, combine soy sauce, honey, and salt. Add this mixture to skillet and combine.

4. Arrange lettuce on a large platter. Slice the chicken and arrange it over the lettuce. Pour sauce over the chicken and serve.

ONE SERVING: 297 Calories; 14.1 grams Fat (2.3 Saturated); 83 mg Cholesterol.

BREAST OF CHICKEN POACHED WITH FRESH VEGETABLES AND FINE HERBS

Holiday magazine considers the Maisonette in Cincinnati, Ohio, to be "one of the finest restaurants in the world," and has awarded them their Award for Dining Distinction for thirty-seven consecutive years. Georges Haidon is the executive chef.

4 Servings
Preparation Time: 15 minutes
Cooking Time: 45 minutes

1 qt. defatted chicken broth	16 thin slices red bell pepper
1 lb. boneless, skinless chicken breasts	8 radishes
4 baby carrots	1 tsp. salt
4 baby turnips	1 tsp. pepper
4 broccoli florets	2 tbsp. chopped parsley
4 cauliflower florets	2 tbsp. minced chives
8 snow peas	2 tbsp. chopped fresh basil
16 thin slices celery	

1. In a large soup pot, bring chicken broth to a boil. Add chicken breasts, reduce heat slightly, and cook until almost tender, about 20 minutes. Add all vegetables, salt, and pepper. Cook until vegetables are crisply tender. Remove chicken and vegetables and keep warm.

2. Continue cooking the stock until it is reduced by half. Check seasoning and add more salt and pepper if necessary. Add parsley, chives, and basil.

3. To serve, place a chicken breast on each serving plate, arrange the vegetables around it, and pour sauce over all.

ONE SERVING: 230 Calories; 5.0 grams Fat (1.4 Saturated); 83 mg Cholesterol.

CHICKEN WITH
MUSTARD-YOGURT SAUCE

"I capture the natural flavors of meat without sautéing in gobs of butter, and stir up a simple low-fat sauce right in the pan," says Chef Emile Mooser of Emile's in San Jose, California. Emile's was chosen "Number One In San Jose" in *Peninsula* magazine's "Ultimate Guide to Dining."

4 Servings
Preparation Time: 8 minutes
Cooking Time: 15 minutes

4 boneless, skinless chicken breasts (16 oz. after trimming)	½ cup defatted chicken stock
2 tbsp. olive oil	¼ cup Dijon mustard
	¼ cup nonfat yogurt
	2 tbsp. slivered chives or green onion tops

1. Separate the tenderloin from each breast. Cut the remaining part of each breast in half lengthwise to make a total of 12 roughly equal pieces. Place the pieces between sheets of wax paper or plastic wrap, and pound to an even thickness.

2. In a large, non-stick frying pan, heat the oil over medium heat. Add the chicken and sauté until browned on both sides, 2 to 3 minutes per side. Transfer the chicken to a plate and keep warm.

3. Pour off any excess oil. Add the chicken stock to the pan and cook over high heat, stirring often, until reduced by half, about 3 minutes. Remove from the heat; then whisk in mustard and yogurt. Add chives or green onion tops.

4. Return chicken to pan to coat with sauce, then serve.

ONE SERVING: 170 Calories; 4.1 grams Fat; 66 mg Cholesterol.

VARIATION: Try this recipe with lean pork or veal loin instead of chicken or experiment with different herbs and mustards.

NICE WITH: Toasted half-circles of low-fat pita bread. Each round loaf boasts four grams of protein, fifty-seven grams of complex carbohydrates, and only seventy calories.

LEMON PEPPER CHICKEN

Lemon may be a chicken's best friend, as in this tangy classic from Chef Robert Mignola of the Post House in New York City. This upscale steak house has been given the *Wine Spectator* award for their outstanding wine list.

4 Servings
Preparation Time: 15 minutes
Marinate: 2 hours
Cooking Time: 45 minutes

½ cup fresh lemon juice
4 cloves garlic, minced
4 shallots, minced
8 fresh thyme sprigs
2 tbsp. olive oil
2 bay leaves

2 2-lb. chickens, skin removed and halved
2 tbsp. freshly grated lemon zest
1 tbsp. coarsely ground black pepper
salt to taste

1. Preheat oven to 450 degrees.

2. In a large shallow bowl, whisk together the lemon juice, garlic, shallots, thyme, and olive oil. Add bay leaves. Place chicken in bowl, turning to coat with the marinade. Marinate, covered, in refrigerator for 2 hours.

3. Arrange chicken on a rack in a roasting pan, and sprinkle with the lemon zest, pepper, and salt to taste. Roast in the middle of a preheated 450-degree oven for 35 to 45 minutes, or until a meat thermometer inserted into the fleshy part of the thigh registers 180 degrees, and the juices run clear when the thigh is pierced with a skewer.

ONE SERVING: 372 Calories; 22.7 grams Fat (4.3 Saturated); 121 mg Cholesterol.

CUBAN CHICKEN MOJO

This is chicken to the tenth power—a perfect introduction to the New World food excitement of Cuban cooking—served to lucky Miami diners at Yuca. According to Chef Douglas Rodriguez, "Cubans normally use mojo sparingly, as it is very spicy."

4 Servings
Preparation Time: 30 minutes
Marinate: Overnight
Cooking Time: 15 minutes

1 tbsp. black peppercorns
1 tbsp. mustard seed
2 tbsp. chopped fresh
    basil, stems removed
2 tbsp. chopped fresh
    cilantro, stems
    removed
2 tbsp. chopped fresh
    parsley, stems
    removed
1 cup diced sweet yellow
    onion (Bermuda or
    Vidalia)

1 bunch scallions, diced
1 cup extra virgin olive oil
1 tbsp. salt
juice of 3 limes
2 chickens, deboned and
    quartered (or
    4 boneless chicken
    breasts)
8 tablespoons Mojo
    Sauce (see recipe)

1. In a food processor or blender, purée all ingredients except chicken and Mojo sauce. Cover chicken with puréed marinade, cover, and refrigerate overnight.

2. The next day, preheat oven to broil, discard marinade, and broil chicken for 15 minutes.

3. Serve with Mojo Sauce on the side.

ONE SERVING (With Mojo Sauce): 422 Calories; 19.3 grams Fat (3.3 Saturated); 119 mg Cholesterol.

NICE WITH: Choose from the classic Cuban accompaniments: yellow rice, sautéed plantains, or black beans.

Mojo Sauce:

1 small red onion, diced
1 tbsp. chopped fresh
    thyme, stems
    removed
1 tbsp. chopped fresh
    oregano, stems
    removed

juice of 2 oranges
juice of 2 limes
juice of 2 lemons
salt and pepper to taste

1. Place all sauce ingredients in blender or food processor and pulse on and off until well blended. Marinate overnight in refrigerator.

2. Next day, bring sauce to room temperature before serving.

NOTE: A mild, dry goat cheese may be substituted for the cotija.

NICE WITH: Chef Sackett serves the enchiladas with her Zocalo Black Beans and a salad of mixed field greens with grated radish in a simple sherry vinaigrette.

ENCHILADAS VERDES

At Zocalo in Philadelphia, ethnic cooking has been elevated to new heights of excellence. For the Mexican specialties, Chef Lou Sackett insists on fresh organic produce, free-range chickens, and handmade tortillas. Try her recipe for these tomatillo-sauced enchiladas with *Zocalo Black Beans.*

4 Servings
Preparation Time: 15 minutes
Cooking Time: 1 hour

1½ lb. fresh tomatillos,
    husked and washed
12 oz. fresh poblano
    chiles
½ cup chopped white
    onion
½ tbsp. chopped garlic
2 tbsp. corn oil
1½ cups natural chicken
    stock

kosher salt
sugar
4 cups lightly cooked,
    shredded chicken
12 thick, white corn
    tortillas (fresh and
    pliable)
1 cup cotija cheese,
    crumbled
½ cup chopped cilantro

1. Poach the tomatillos in barely simmering water until just softened and their color turns olive green, about 10 minutes. Drain, refresh under cold water, and place in blender.

2. Place poblano chiles directly over gas flame (or on a charcoal grill), turning often, until blackened all over. Don't overcook the flesh. Place in a plastic bag, allow to cool gradually, then scrape off charred skin. Stem, seed, and devein the chiles and add to tomatillos in blender.

3. Add onion and garlic to blender. Blend, adding as little water as possible, to make a smooth purée.

4. Heat a large, non-aluminum saucepan until it is very hot. Add 2 tablespoons of corn oil, then pour in tomatillo purée. (Stand back to avoid hot splatters.) Cook over high heat, stirring constantly, for about 3 minutes, or until slightly reduced and flavors are blended. Add chicken stock, cook for about 8 to 10 minutes, and reduce to a medium-thick sauce. Add pinches of salt and sugar as needed to balance the flavors.

5. Preheat oven to 400 degrees. Combine chicken with ¾ cup tomatillo sauce.

6. Heat one tortilla over a gas flame or in a dry sauté pan until very pliable. Dip on both sides in tomatillo sauce and place on a plate. Place a strip of chicken across the tortilla, roll up, and place in a baking dish. Repeat, filling all twelve tortillas as quickly as possible. Nap edges with sauce. Keep remaining sauce hot. Immediately place enchiladas in oven and bake for 10 to 15 minutes, or until heated thorough.

7. Place 3 enchiladas on each of 4 hot plates. Top with remaining sauce. Garnish each trio of enchiladas with one diagonal stripe of crumbled cotija cheese and a parallel stripe of chopped cilantro.

ONE SERVING: 460 Calories; 19.3 grams Fat (6.4 Saturated); 97 mg Cholesterol.

NOTE: Found in most spice sections, bouquet garni is a blend of oregano, summer savory, marjoram, rosemary, basil, thyme, dill, and tarragon.

LE SUPREME DE POULET A LA PROVENÇALE

California chef, Jean-Pierre Martinez, has a way with French bistro cuisine that comes quite naturally. After stringent years of training and experience in his native France, he was designated a master chef. Jean-Pierre and his wife, well-known restauranteur Jeanne Driscoll, oversee the Piret restaurant as well as Palmier Bistro in San Diego.

4 Servings
Preparation Time: 15 minutes
Cooking Time: 20 minutes

3 tbsp. extra virgin olive oil
4 6-oz. boneless, skinless chicken breasts
½ cup sliced onion
4 small tomatoes, finely diced
1 tbsp. minced garlic
1 tbsp. minced shallots
1 tsp. bouquet garni
½ cup water
salt and pepper to taste
1 cup minced fresh basil

1. In a sauté pan, heat 2 tablespoons olive oil and brown the chicken for 3 to 4 minutes per side. Set aside.

2. In a large saucepan over medium heat, heat 1 tablespoon olive oil. Add onion and cook until lightly golden, about 5 minutes. Add tomatoes, garlic, shallots, bouquet garni, water, salt, and pepper. Bring to a boil, reduce heat, and simmer for about 12 minutes. Add basil. Return chicken to pan to warm and serve.

ONE SERVING: 348 Calories; 15.4 grams Fat (2.8 Saturated); 107 mg Cholesterol.

GRILLED CHICKEN WITH SALAD AND FRESH HERBS

This speedy entree from Faces Trattoria in New York City is delicately seasoned and artfully presented.

4 Servings
Preparation Time: 15 minutes
Cooking Time: 15 minutes

1 head radicchio, in bite-sized pieces
1 bunch arugula
1 Belgian endive, in bite-sized pieces
1 tomato, coarsely chopped
16 oz. skinless, boneless chicken breasts

4 tbsp. extra-virgin olive oil
1 tbsp. chopped fresh rosemary leaves
1 tbsp. fresh oregano leaves
3 tbsp. balsamic vinegar
salt and pepper

1. Preheat grill.

2. In a large bowl, combine radicchio, arugula, endive, and tomato.

3. Split the chicken breasts, slice thin on the diagonal, and season with salt and pepper. Toss with 1 tablespoon olive oil. Arrange chicken strips side-by-side on a platter. Slide them onto preheated grill with a spatula. Grill, about 4 inches from coals, for 3 to 4 minutes, turning once, until just cooked through. Transfer chicken to a clean bowl. Add rosemary and oregano and toss to coat the chicken well.

4. Place vinegar in a small saucepan; then whisk in the remaining 3 tablespoons olive oil. Add salt and pepper to taste. Heat the dressing over low heat just until warm.

5. Divide the salad among 4 plates, arrange the chicken on top, whisk the warm dressing well, and drizzle it over each serving.

ONE SERVING: 297 Calories; 17.7 grams Fat (2.9 Saturated); 83 mg Cholesterol.

VARIATION: Try substituting two tablespoons fresh tarragon leaves for the rosemary and oregano.

NICE WITH: Lightly sautéed shitake mushrooms, sourdough French bread, and a chilled Sauvignon Blanc.

NOTE: Ask your butcher to bone and separate the duck meat from the skin. You should have four skinless fillets ready to be marinated and grilled.

NICE WITH: Noodles cooked in chicken broth and a heady California Cabernet.

HEALTH TIP: Enjoy the rich taste of duck knowing that it has about the same calorie and fat content as dark meat of chicken.

BREAST OF DUCK WITH RASPBERRY-BLACK BEAN GASTRIQUE

Chef R. Michael Stanley oversees the kitchen at The Lark and The Dove, an Atlanta landmark restaurant. The unusual combination of tastes in this signature dish will have your guests trying to identify the ingredients and begging for the recipe!

4 Servings
Preparation Time: 40 minutes

1 cup fresh lime juice	½ cup cooked black beans
1 cup apple purée or unsweetened applesauce	1 tbsp. molasses
4 tbsp. olive oil	1 tbsp. dark brown sugar
4 5-oz. boneless duck breasts	¼ tsp. poppy seeds
½ pint fresh raspberries	⅛ tsp. ground coriander
	2 peeled oranges, sliced
	whole raspberries for garnish

1. Preheat grill.

2. Combine lime juice, apple purée, and oil. Marinate duck for 10 minutes.

3. In a food processor, combine raspberries, black beans, molasses, brown sugar, poppy seeds, and ground coriander. Purée until smooth. Transfer to a saucepan and simmer, stirring, for about 15 minutes.

4. Grill duck until just done. Do not overcook.

5. To serve, slice duck at an angle. On a plate, fan orange slices and place duck over oranges. Top with gastrique sauce and garnish with whole raspberries.

ONE SERVING: 201 Calories; 11.6 grams Fat (0.1 Saturated); 89 mg Cholesterol.

CORNISH GAME HEN WITH ORANGE APRICOT SAUCE

At Ivy's in San Francisco, Chef Rick Cunningham serves this delectable dish with *Wild Rice Compote*. Ivy's is where many San Francisco diners head before or after attending a concert at the nearby Performing Arts Center.

6 Servings
Preparation Time: 30 minutes
Marinate: At least 4 hours
Cooking Time: 40 minutes

3 Cornish game hens,
   cleaned and halved
4 cups fresh orange juice
2 tbsp. white wine vinegar
1 tbsp. molasses
2 tsp. minced garlic
1 tbsp. minced ginger
2 cinnamon sticks
1 tbsp. plus 2 tsp. olive
   oil

4 shallots, sliced
1 cup chicken stock
2 tsp. cornstarch
2 tsp. cold water
1 cup julienned leeks,
   white part only
1 cup julienned dried
   apricots
salt and pepper

1. Combine 2 cups of the orange juice with the vinegar, molasses, garlic, ginger, and cinnamon sticks. Marinate hens in this mixture for at least 4 hours, turning occasionally. Remove hens, reserving marinade, and roast at 425 degrees for 10 minutes. Reduce heat to 350 degrees and continue roasting until juices run clear when the thickest part of thigh is pierced, about 30 minutes. (Hens can also be cooked on a grill.)

2. In a large, heavy saucepan, heat 1 tablespoon olive oil. Add shallots and sauté until golden brown, about 3 minutes. Add remaining orange juice, chicken stock, and the reserved marinade (discard cinnamon). Bring to a boil, then simmer for 20 minutes.

3. Combine cornstarch and water; then add to sauce. Simmer 5 minutes more.

HEALTH TIP: The fruit in this dish provides a whopping 130 percent of the daily requirement of vitamin C. Paired with the protein-rich, low-fat game hen, each serving is a nutritional bargain.

NICE WITH: Accompany with Wild Rice Compote (see index for recipe) or steamed rice, if desired.

4. In a small skillet, heat 1 teaspoon olive oil and sauté the leeks and apricots until the leeks are translucent, 3 to 4 minutes. Season to taste with salt and pepper, then add to sauce.

5. Serve hens with warm sauce spooned over them.

ONE SERVING: 399 Calories; 16.8 grams Fat; 74 mg Cholesterol.

CHICKEN AJILLO IBERIAN

The heady aroma of garlic drifts from the kitchen when this is being prepared at the Spanish restaurant, Iberian, in Huntington, New York. The amount of oil has been slightly reduced in this version.

4 Servings
Preparation Time: 15 minutes
Cooking Time: 40 minutes

3 tbsp. olive oil (Spanish preferable)	⅛ tsp. paprika
12 garlic cloves, peeled	2 chicken breasts
¼ tsp. freshly ground black pepper	2 chicken legs
¼ tsp. cayenne	2 chicken thighs
	¼ cup dry white wine
	saffron rice

1. In a large skillet, heat the oil and add garlic, black pepper, cayenne, paprika, and chicken. Cover the skillet and cook over medium heat for 15 minutes. Turn chicken and continue cooking for 15 more minutes. Drain off all but 1 tablespoon olive oil, add the wine, and cook the chicken, covered, for 1 minute.

2. Transfer the chicken to a serving dish, pour sauce and garlic cloves over all. Serve with saffron rice.

ONE SERVING: 462 Calories; 24.7 grams Fat (4.9 Saturated); 168 mg Cholesterol.

NICE WITH: A well-balanced, light red wine from the El Bierzo region of Spain would complement this dish nicely. It is interesting to note that Spain has more land under vines than any other country. Much of their wine, however, is not exported.

BREAST OF PHEASANT WITH CELERY ROOT AND CRANBERRY-PEPPER SAUCE

For Thanksgiving, try this recipe from Pascal Vignau using pheasant or fresh turkey breast. The savory combination of healthy ingredients could easily replace the fat-laden traditional fare. Chef Vignau is the award-winning chef at the Ritz Carlton in Chicago, which was named "Best Hotel Dining Room" by *Chicago* magazine.

8 Servings
Preparation Time: 15 minutes
Cooking Time: 35 minutes

1½ cups fresh
    cranberries
½ cup white wine
8 cups rich pheasant,
    chicken, or turkey
    stock
2 tbsp. cracked black
    pepper
sugar substitute
    (optional)
3 fresh celery roots,
    peeled and diced

1 tbsp. olive oil
8 6-oz. skinless, boneless
    breasts of pheasant,
    turkey, or chicken
1 tbsp. butter
16 oz. large white
    mushrooms, thickly
    sliced
calorie-reduced margarine
    (optional)

1. In a saucepan over medium heat, cook cranberries until they crack open, 1 to 2 minutes. Add wine and cook for 5 minutes. Add 3 cups of stock and the cracked pepper. Cook for 15 minutes over low heat, until reduced to a medium-thick sauce. (It will be quite tart.) Add sugar substitute if desired.

2. Meanwhile, in a large saucepan, heat the remaining 5 cups of stock. Add diced celery root and cook until tender, about 8 minutes. Drain, reserving cooking liquid. Transfer cooked celery root to a blender or food processor and blend until smooth. (It may be necessary to add a little cooking liquid to make a smooth purée.) Add salt and pepper to taste. Add calorie-reduced margarine if desired.

HEALTH TIP: Commercially raised pheasant is a white-fleshed bird, more lean (and less gamey-tasting) than its wild counterpart.

NOTE: Celery root looks like a dark, knobby turnip. Unknown to most American cooks, they are sometimes tossed in the exotic vegetable bin and forgotten by the grocer. Because celery root tends to be expensive, make sure it is acceptably fresh. If in doubt, ask to have one cut in half. The white root should not look excessively woody, nor have a black center. You should smell the pleasing aroma of the celery.

3. Heat butter and olive oil in a heavy skillet over medium heat. Add the pheasant breasts and sear on both sides until tender, about 5 minutes. Remove pheasant, drain, and keep warm. Add mushrooms and cook until soft and brown, about 3 minutes.

4. To serve, make a circle of mushrooms in center of each plate, fill with celery root purée, top with sliced pheasant and cranberry pepper sauce. Serve remaining sauce on the side.

ONE SERVING: 319 Calories; 10.9 grams Fat (1.1 Saturated); 0 mg Cholesterol.

CAST IRON SEARED AND ROASTED PHEASANT

Chef David Foegley is creating midwestern magic at the contemporary restaurant called Peter's in Indianapolis, Indiana.

4 Servings
Preparation Time: 40 minutes

1 tbsp. ground sage	4 boned pheasant halves
1 tbsp. ground savory	2 tbsp. olive oil
1 tbsp. ground thyme	12 spears asparagus
1 tbsp. salt	8 baby beets
1 tsp. ground white pepper	

1. Preheat oven to 425 degrees.

2. In a small bowl, combine sage, savory, thyme, salt, and white pepper. Dust each pheasant half with seasoning mixture, then shake off excess.

3. Heat a cast iron skillet until very hot, then add olive oil. Add pheasant and sear on all sides until lightly browned. Transfer to a roasting pan and roast at 425 degrees for 20 minutes.

HINT: Pheasant is a tasty bird that deserves more of our culinary attention. Ask your butcher for the plumpest, commercially raised game bird available.

VARIATION: Use unboned pheasant breasts or try turkey or chicken breasts.

NICE WITH: Various steamed vegetables and old-fashioned mashed potatoes.

4. Meanwhile, cook asparagus and beets in separate pans of boiling water until tender.

5. To serve, slice pheasant and arrange on plate with vegetables. Pour pan juices over pheasant as a sauce.

ONE SERVING: 396 Calories; 11.3 grams Fat (2.4 Saturated); NA Cholesterol.

GRILLED CHICKEN WITH HONEY, LIME, AND GARLIC GLAZE

Another winner from Yuca in Miami. This sauce is equally good brushed on grilled fish, turkey breast, or Rock Cornish game hens. Chef Douglas Rodriguez says, "The ideas for new dishes just come to me. I just start putting things together. Sometimes, the dish will need more color or spice— but the idea is to combine different textures and flavors of simple foods into a complex dish."

4 Servings
Preparation Time: 25 minutes

⅓ cup fresh lime juice
2 tbsp. honey
4 garlic cloves, chopped
1 small serrano or
     jalapeno chili, seeded
     and minced
1 canned chipotle chili in
     adobo sauce
¼ tsp. cornstarch
1 tbsp. minced fresh
     cilantro
4 6-oz. boneless, skinless
     chicken breasts

NOTE: Chipotle chiles in adobo sauce are available at Latin food markets and some specialty grocery stores.

1. Preheat grill.

2. In a food processor or blender, purée first 6 ingredients. Transfer mixture to a saucepan. Boil until slightly thickened, about 1 minute, then stir in cilantro.

3. Brush chicken breasts lightly with glaze. Grill for about 4 minutes on each side, turning once. Just before removing from grill, baste the breasts with the remainder of the glaze.

ONE SERVING: 296 Calories; 6.4 grams Fat; 121 mg Cholesterol.

Meat

Meat

Sesame Beef with Asian Vinaigrette
Spiced Lamb Shanks with Eggplant
Joe's Greek Special
Roast Pork Tenderloin with Lemon Pear Chutney
Veal Medallions with Creamy Chive Sauce
Sautéed Venison Medallions with Whidbey's Port Demi-glace
and Roasted Elephant Garlic
Poached Beef Filets on Fresh Horseradish Sauce
Braised Veal Shanks
Grilled Lamb with Vegetables, Rosemary Rice,
and Balsamic Vinaigrette
Roast Pork with Fruit Compote
Tenderloin of Beef in a Gingered Brandy-Mustard Sauce
Chico's Chili
Veal Medallions with Braised Endives and Boiled Potatoes
Lamb Spirals with Pine Nuts and Garlic
Piri-Piri Vinaigrette (for Grilled Steak)
Garlic, Lemon, Olive, and Mint Compote (for Pork or Lamb)
Cabernet Cassis Sauce (for Beef or Veal)

SESAME BEEF WITH ASIAN VINAIGRETTE

San Francisco Bay ferry passengers often make a stop in Sausalito to dine at the Victorian restaurant, Casa Madrona. Here's one of their most requested recipes—a quick stir-fry with the exotic taste of Pan-Asian cuisine.

4 Servings
Preparation Time: 15 minutes
Marinating Time: At least one hour
Cooking Time: 5 minutes

½ cup plus 2 tbsp. sodium-reduced soy sauce
1½ tbsp. chopped fresh ginger
4 cloves garlic, minced
½ cup chopped cilantro
1 lb. flank steak
½ cup plus 1 tsp. olive oil
¼ cup balsamic vinegar

1 tbsp. sesame oil
freshly ground pepper
¾ lb. (about 4 cups) bitter greens (endive, arugula, bok choy, radicchio), washed and torn into bite-sized pieces
2 tbsp. toasted sesame seeds

1. Combine ½ cup soy sauce with ginger, garlic, and cilantro to make a marinade.

2. Trim meat of all fat and cut across the grain into ¼-inch strips. Toss beef with marinade, then marinate for at least one hour.

3. Mix together vinegar, sesame oil, ground pepper, ½ cup olive oil, and 2 tablespoons soy sauce with a wire whisk.

4. Arrange greens on eight plates.

5. Remove beef from marinade. In a skillet or wok, heat 1 teaspoon olive oil over high heat, then sear the meat quickly. Immediately place beef on top of greens, then add vinaigrette mixture to the same pan. Cook and stir for 1 minute, scraping pan. Pour a portion of hot vinaigrette over each plate. Sprinkle with sesame seeds and serve.

PER SERVING: 376 Calories; 26 grams Fat (5 Saturated); 68 mg Cholesterol.

SPICED LAMB SHANKS WITH EGGPLANT

Redolent of garlic and herbs, this may be lamb shank's finest hour. It's just one of Gordon Hamersley's creations that has Bostonians flocking to Hamersley's Bistro.

4 Servings
Preparation Time: 1 hour
Cooking Time: 2½ hours

1 eggplant (about 1 lb.), peeled and cut into 1-inch cubes
1 tsp. salt
1 tbsp. ground coriander
1 tbsp. ground cumin
1½ tsp. herbes de Provence
1½ tsp. freshly ground black pepper
1½ tsp. ground ginger
½ tsp. turmeric
4 lamb shanks (about 2¾ lb.), trimmed
4 tsp. vegetable oil

3 carrots, peeled and cut into 2-inch lengths
1 onion, sliced
1 head garlic, separated and peeled
3 cups dry red wine (or one 750 ml bottle)
2½ cups chicken stock or water
⅓ cup fresh orange juice
1 tbsp. tomato paste
1 tbsp. chopped fresh mint
fresh mint springs (for garnish)

1. Preheat oven to 325 degrees.

2. Place eggplant in a colander over a bowl. Sprinkle with salt and let stand for 30 minutes. Rinse eggplant and pat it dry.

3. In a shallow dish, combine coriander, cumin, herbes de Provence, pepper, ginger, and tumeric. Roll lamb shanks in the spice mixture, pressing spices evenly into the meat.

4. In a large, non-stick skillet, heat 2 teaspoons oil over medium-high heat. Cook shanks, in batches if necessary, until evenly browned. Transfer to a 6-quart roasting pan.

5. To the skillet, add eggplant, carrots, onion, and whole garlic cloves. Cook over medium heat, stirring, for 3 to 5 minutes, or until softened; then add the vegetables to the roasting pan.

NOTE: Herbes de Provence is a spice mixture found in specialty food markets. You can make your own by combining equal parts of fennel seed, sage, rosemary, marjoram, thyme, and savory.

MAKE AHEAD: Prepare entire recipe up to three days in advance and reheat.

6. In the same skillet, combine the wine, stock, orange juice, tomato paste, and mint. Bring to a boil while stirring; then pour the liquid over shanks and vegetables. Cover and bake in a 350-degree oven for about 2 hours, or until shanks are very tender. Transfer the meat and vegetables to a serving platter; cover and keep warm. Skim fat from remaining liquid in roasting pan.

7. Transfer skimmed liquid from roasting pan to a saucepan. Bring to a boil and cook for 3 to 5 minutes, or until slightly thickened. Taste and adjust seasonings. Spoon a small amount of the sauce over the shanks and vegetables. Garnish the platter with mint sprigs. Serve remaining sauce separately at the table.

ONE SERVING: 267 Calories; 11 grams Fat (4.3 Saturated); 63 mg Cholesterol.

JOE'S GREEK SPECIAL

Some people believe that a trip to San Francisco is not complete without a stop at Original Joe's for the famous "Special"—a beefy spinach omelet. This version subtracts cholesterol and adds spice.

4 Servings
Preparation Time: 40 minutes

4 pita bread rounds, split
   horizontally and
   toasted
1 10-oz. pkg. frozen
   chopped spinach
spray cooking oil
1 cup chopped onion
2 garlic cloves, minced
1 lb. lean ground beef
1 tsp. oregano
dash cinnamon

½ tsp. salt
1 tsp. pepper
4 tbsp. grated parmesan
   cheese
2 tbsp. toasted pine nuts
2 oz. feta cheese,
   crumbled
¼ cup plain low-fat
   yogurt
1 egg, beaten

NICE WITH: Greek olives and a broiled tomato half that has been sprinkled with oregano and red wine vinegar.

HEALTH TIP: Obtaining the required amount of calcium, at least 800 milligrams per day, can be difficult. In this recipe, the spinach, feta, parmesan, and yogurt each supply a hefty amount of the bone-building nutrient.

1. Cook spinach. Drain well and set aside.

2. Spray a large skillet with cooking oil. Add onions and garlic; then cook until onions are soft. Add beef and sauté until no longer pink. Add oregano, cinnamon, salt, pepper, 2 tablespoons parmesan cheese, pine nuts, feta cheese, yogurt, and the drained spinach. Stir until well blended.

3. Using a fork, blend the beaten egg into the mixture. Cook for 2 or 3 minutes.

4. On each plate, place ½ toasted pita round and top with beef-spinach mixture. Sprinkle with the remaining parmesan cheese. Cut remaining toasted pita rounds into wedges and serve on the side.

ONE SERVING: 465 calories; 21.8 grams Fat; (6.7 Saturated); 137 mg Cholesterol.

ROAST PORK TENDERLOIN WITH LEMON PEAR CHUTNEY

At the King Cole, this succulent pork is served with *Wild Rice Cakes*—a knock-out combination that will impress your choosiest guests. If you don't think of Dayton, Ohio as mecca for food lovers, think again! This is the upscale sort of cooking excitement that Chef Steven Hunn creates daily at the King Cole.

4 Servings
Preparation Time: 20 minutes
Marinate: 2 hours
Cooking Time: 1 hour

VARIATION: Pork may be grilled over medium-hot coals and brushed with the marinade as it cooks.

MAKE AHEAD: The chutney can be made several days in advance.

4 cloves garlic, minced
5 bay leaves
½ tsp. marjoram
¼ tsp. thyme
salt and coarsely ground
    black pepper
5 tbsp. olive oil
2 tbsp. balsamic vinegar
2 lb. pork tenderloin,
    trimmed of all fat
½ cup minced onion
½ cup golden raisins

2 tbsp. fresh grated
    ginger
1 cup sugar
1 cup water
1 cup cider vinegar
zest from 2 small lemons
juice from 2 small
    lemons
1 cinnamon stick
3 pears, peeled, cored,
    and diced
½ cup sliced almonds

1. In a bowl, combine garlic, 4 bay leaves, marjoram, thyme, salt, and pepper. Whisk in balsamic vinegar and 4 tablespoons oil. Pour mixture over pork in a shallow container and marinate for 2 hours.

2. In a large, heavy-bottomed saucepan over medium heat, add remaining 1 tablespoon olive oil, then cook onions just until translucent. Add raisins, ginger, sugar, water, cider vinegar, lemon zest, lemon juice, cinnamon stick, and remaining bay leaf. Simmer for about 30 minutes or until the liquid is syrupy. Add the pears and simmer just until tender. (Ripe pears require only 1 or 2 minutes.) Remove bay leaf and cinnamon stick. Allow to cool, then stir in the almonds.

3. Preheat oven to 325 degrees. In a heavy-bottomed, ovenproof skillet over medium heat, sear the whole pork tenderloin until browned all over. Season with salt and pepper and place in the preheated oven for about 15 minutes, or until an internal temperature of 150 degrees is reached. Slice and serve with the chutney.

ONE SERVING (With 2 tbsp. chutney): 486 Calories; 24.9 grams Fat (7.4 Saturated); 140 mg Cholesterol.

VEAL MEDALLIONS WITH CREAMY CHIVE SAUCE

Lightly-sautéed veal is topped with a spinach-chive sauce that's ready in twenty minutes—all for only 156 calories. Fio Antognini teaches the techniques of healthy cooking and demonstrates the step-by-step preparation of low-calorie gourmet meals on his own video. He is the chef and owner of Fio's in St. Louis, Missouri.

4 Servings
Preparation Time: 10 minutes
Cooking Time: 10 minutes

4 tbsp. plain low-fat
    yogurt
4 tbsp. low-fat cottage
    cheese
4 tbsp. low-fat ricotta
    cheese
½ cup fresh chives,
    chopped
16 large spinach leaves
1 tsp. sodium-reduced
    soy sauce
splash lemon juice

splash dry sherry
1 lb. veal medallions
    (weighed after
    trimming fat)
freshly ground pepper
paprika
cooking oil spray
4 large mushrooms,
    quartered
4 purple kale leaves for
    garnish

1. In a food processor or blender, blend yogurt, cottage cheese, ricotta cheese, chives, spinach, soy sauce, lemon juice and sherry. Transfer to a saucepan or microwave-safe bowl and warm gently.

2. Season veal with pepper and paprika. Spray a non-stick skillet with oil. Sauté veal and mushrooms until veal is lightly browned and mushrooms are tender, about 4 minutes.

3. Pour sauce over veal. Serve garnished with kale leaves.

ONE SERVING: 156 Calories; 5.3 grams Fat; 115 mg Cholesterol.

HEALTH TIP: For ricotta cheese with the lowest fat content, choose a brand that has been imported from Italy. There, ricotta is made from whey, the liquid drained off in the process of making higher fat cheeses such as provolone. The whey is then heated to produce the moist, slightly sweet cheese called ricotta, or "recooked." Some American brands of ricotta contain a combination of whey and whole milk, and they are not as low in fat as the Italian ricotta.

NOTE: *If Whidbey's port is not available, any high-quality port may be used.*

HINT: *The milder-flavored bulbs of elephant garlic are easier to peel and chop than their smaller cousins.*

SAUTEED VENISON MEDALLIONS WITH WHIDBEY'S PORT DEMI-GLACE AND ROASTED ELEPHANT GARLIC

Chef Barbara Figueroa has shared one of her signature dishes—lean venison in a sensational wine sauce. The menu at Seattle's Hunt Club in the Sorrento Hotel features the cuisine of the Pacific Northwest. *Money* magazine named it one of the "Top Three Restaurants in Seattle." Chef Figueroa is on the elite James Beard Foundation list of "America's Best Chefs."

6 Servings
Preparation Time: 15 minutes
Roasting Time: 1 hour
Final Cooking Time: 25 minutes

**6 cloves elephant garlic,
   peeled**
6 tbsp. olive oil
salt and pepper
**1 qt. venison or veal
   stock**
1¼ cups ruby port
1 cup chopped onion
½ cup chopped carrot
½ cup chopped celery
1 tsp. chopped thyme

1 tsp. chopped sage
2 juniper berries, crushed
1 clove garlic, minced
2 tbsp. Whidbey's port
½ tsp. red wine vinegar
**2¼ lb. boneless loin of
   venison, cut into
   12 medallions**
2 tbsp. chopped chives
**fresh thyme or sage
   leaves for garnish**

1. Preheat oven to 325 degrees.

2. In a heavy-bottomed skillet combine garlic and 2 tablespoons olive oil. Season with salt and pepper. Cover skillet tightly with foil. Place in 325-degree oven. Roast for 1 hour, or until garlic is easily pierced with a fork.

3. In a medium saucepan, combine stock, ruby port, onion, carrot, celery, thyme, sage, juniper berries, and garlic. Cook over medium heat until mixture is reduced by ¼, or until sauce is thick enough to coat a spoon. Strain through a fine mesh strainer. Whisk in 2 tablespoons olive oil, Whidbey's port, and red wine vinegar.

4. In a heavy skillet, heat 2 tablespoons olive oil until almost smoking. Season venison medallions with salt and pepper. Add enough venison to fill skillet without crowding. Sauté, turning once, until well seared outside and rare inside. Repeat with remaining medallions, adding a little more oil if necessary.

5. To serve, ladle demi-glace onto plate. Arrange two venison medallions on each plate. Cut roasted garlic cloves into fan shapes or slices. Arrange one on each plate and sprinkle with chives. Garnish with a sprig of fresh thyme or sage.

ONE SERVING: 404 Calories; 24.1 grams Fat (4.3 Saturated); NA Cholesterol.

POACHED BEEF FILETS ON FRESH HORSERADISH SAUCE

This elegant method of preparing beef will be a treasure to any calorie counter who is also a hostess. It comes from Dominique Jamain of the Maile Restaurant at the award-winning Kahala Hilton in Honolulu, Hawaii.

6 Servings
Preparation Time: 15 minutes
Cooking Time: 20 minutes

6 5-oz. beef filets
24 oz. beef stock
12 black peppercorns, crushed
1 bouquet garni (celery, leek, carrots, onion)
salt and pepper

Horseradish Sauce:

8 oz. beef stock
4 oz. light cream
8 oz. white wine
½ cup finely chopped mushrooms

⅓ cup finely chopped leeks
½ cup finely chopped celery
¼ cup fresh horseradish root, finely grated
1 tbsp. unsalted butter
salt and white pepper
additional grated horseradish root (optional)

HINT: For the bouquet garni, Chef Jamain uses the classic method of chopping vegetables and bundling them in a square of knotted cheesecloth.

VARIATION: The horseradish sauce is equally delicious with beef tenderloin that has been grilled over hot coals and then sliced thinly across the grain.

1. Place beef filets in simmering beef stock with bouquet garni, salt and pepper, making sure beef is completely covered with stock. Simmer until required doneness is reached (10 to 11 minutes for medium). Remove filets from stock and let rest for a few minutes before slicing.

2. In a large saucepan, combine stock, cream, wine, mushrooms, leeks, and celery. Bring to a boil, then cook over medium-high heat until mixture is reduced by half. Add ¼ cup grated horseradish and cook for 3 minutes more. Strain.

3. Place sauce in blender, add butter, and blend at high speed. Season with salt and pepper to taste. (If a hotter sauce is desired, add extra grated horseradish.) Serve over sliced filets.

ONE SERVING (With 2 tbsp. sauce): 275 Calories; 13.6 grams Fat (6.1 Saturated); 103 mg Cholesterol.

BRAISED VEAL SHANKS

Here's another technique for healthy cooking from Emile Mooser: "Braising is a classic way of roasting with moisture so meat comes out fork-tender. To keep this dish lean, I skip the flouring step and always trim away all visible fat." Mooser always serves this well-sauced veal with his creamy *New-Way Risotto*.

4 Servings
Preparation Time: 30 minutes
Cooking Time: About 2 hours

1 navel orange	½ cup chopped carrots
4 veal shanks of equal size, 1½ inches thick (2 lb. total)	4 to 5 cups defatted stock
	1 bay leaf
2 tsp. olive oil	pinch ground white pepper
1 cup chopped onions	2 tbsp. minced fresh basil
½ cup chopped shallots	

MAKE AHEAD: The entire recipe can be made ahead of time and reheated. It also freezes well.

NICE WITH: The veal is especially nice with a creamy risotto.

1. Preheat oven to 350 degrees.

2. Working over a bowl to catch juice, peel and section the orange, discarding thin membranes between sections. Set aside sections and any collected juice.

3. Trim veal of all visible fat. In a large, oven-proof skillet over medium heat, sauté veal until well browned, about 5 minutes per side. Remove.

4. Reduce heat and add the onions, shallots, and carrots. Cook until onions are transluscent, about 20 minutes. Pour off any fat, then return veal to pan.

5. Add 4 cups of stock and bay leaf. Cover skillet and transfer to oven. Bake at 350 degrees for 1¼ to 1½ hours, or until the veal is tender. Remove veal, cover with foil, and keep warm.

6. Return skillet to stove. If necessary, add remaining cup of stock to make about 2 cups. Bring liquid to a boil and reduce by ⅓. Stir in the reserved orange juice and pepper. Discard bay leaf. Return veal to pan and coat well with sauce.

7. Serve veal garnished with reserved orange sections and basil.

ONE SERVING: 340 Calories; 8.4 grams Fat (1.9 Saturated); 94 mg Cholesterol.

GRILLED LAMB WITH VEGETABLES, ROSEMARY RICE, AND BALSAMIC VINAIGRETTE

The Brennan family—Ella, Dick, Dottie, and John—are responsible for the imaginative entrees, such as this savory lamb, served at the legendary Commander's Palace in New Orleans.

4 Servings
Preparation Time: 20 minutes
Cooking Time: 25 minutes

HEALTH TIP: Well-trimmed lamb weighs in at a respectable 54 calories per ounce of cooked meat. Trimming all of the visible fat from any meat, choosing lean cuts, and cooking with a minimum of additional fat allows us to enjoy meat as part of a rational diet.

NICE WITH: Pour a glass of Merlot to complement the pungent herbs and the full-flavored lamb.

1 lb. lean ground lamb
3 tbsp. finely chopped fresh oregano
1 tbsp. finely chopped fresh thyme
3 tsp. finely chopped fresh rosemary
6 grinds fresh black pepper
1 tsp. salt
4 tbsp. extra virgin olive oil
cooking oil spray
1 cup finely chopped yellow onion
1 cup rice
1½ cups water
½ tsp. white pepper
1 tbsp. balsamic vinegar
½ tsp. Dijon mustard
1 tsp. olive oil
2 cups julienned assorted vegetables (carrots, zucchini, red peppers, etc.)

1. Preheat grill (optional).

2. Combine lamb, oregano, thyme, 1 teaspoon rosemary, pepper, salt, and 1 tablespoon olive oil. Form into eight 2-ounce patties. Refrigerate.

3. Spray a small non-stick saucepan with cooking oil spray; then cook onions over medium heat until translucent. Add rice, remaining 2 teaspoons rosemary, water, and white pepper. Bring to a boil, reduce heat, and cover. Cook for 12 minutes. Keep warm.

4. In a small bowl, combine vinegar, mustard, 3 tablespoons olive oil, and salt and white pepper to taste. Reserve at room temperature.

5. In a hot sauté pan, heat 1 teaspoon olive oil. Add julienned vegetables. Cook and stir until barely tender.

6. In a second sauté pan (or on a hot grill) cook the lamb patties to desired doneness, turning once.

7. To serve, place sautéed vegetables on plate. Using a small cup to mold rice, place ¼ of the rice in the center of each plate. Arrange 2 lamb patties around rice and spoon 1 table-spoon vinaigrette over the patties.

ONE SERVING (With rice): 492 Calories; 26.6 grams Fat (7.0 Saturated); 79 mg Cholesterol.

ROAST PORK WITH FRUIT COMPOTE

Chef Emile Mooser says, "To get a low-fat pork roast, I start with a very lean cut of pork—the loin. The roasting method is one hundred percent classic, but I add as little fat as possible—barely a teaspoon sometimes." Emile Mooser has made Emile's one of the most popular restaurants in San Jose, California, by never compromising his belief in serving low-fat, high-nutrition dishes.

4 Servings
Preparation Time: 20 minutes
Marinate: 3-4 hours
Cooking Time: 40 to 50 minutes

1 McIntosh apple, cored
    and quartered
1 Bosc pear, cored and
    quartered
½ cup diced onions
⅓ cup diced carrots
2 bay leaves
1 tbsp. fruit concentrate
1 tbsp. minced fresh
    thyme
2 cloves garlic, minced
1 tbsp. grated orange rind

1½ lb. boneless pork
    loin, trimmed of all
    visible fat
1½ tsp. olive oil
1 cup raspberries
1 cup defatted stock
1 cup apple cider
2 tbsp. cold water
1 tbsp. cornstarch
pinch ground white
    pepper

1. Chop 1 quarter of the apple and 1 quarter of the pear (reserve remaining quarters). Add onions, carrots, bay leaves, fruit concentrate, thyme, garlic, and orange rind. Mix well.

2. Rub pork on all sides with ½ teaspoon olive oil, then coat with fruit marinade. Cover and refrigerate for 3 to 4 hours.

3. Preheat oven to 350 degrees.

4. Coarsely chop the remaining apple and pear quarters. In a saucepan, heat 1 teaspoon olive oil. Add apples and pears and sauté for about 3 minutes. Stir in raspberries, remove from heat, and set aside.

NICE WITH: Chef Mooser likes to serve this dish with polenta croutons. He cuts chilled polenta into thin slices and sautés them in a non-stick frying pan until golden on both sides.

NOTE: Fruit concentrate is available in health food stores.

5. Remove pork from fruit marinade (reserve marinade). In a heavy, ovenproof pan over high heat, sear pork for about 4 minutes per side. Remove pork from pan. Place on a roasting rack that fits inside ovenproof pan. Place reserved fruit marinade on the bottom of the pan.

6. Roast at 350 degrees for 40 to 50 minutes, or until pork reaches an internal temperature of 140 degrees. Remove pork, set aside, and keep warm.

7. Remove accumulated fat from roasting pan. Add stock and cider. Place pan on a burner over high heat. Cook, stirring constantly, for about 5 minutes to deglaze.

8. In a cup, mix the water and cornstarch until smooth. Add to the pan and stir until thickened. Strain the sauce into a saucepan and season with the pepper. Keep warm over low heat.

9. Briefly reheat the compote. Thinly slice pork and serve with compote and sauce.

ONE SERVING: 335 Calories; 6.7 grams Fat; 111 mg Cholesterol.

NICE WITH: A glistening green salad, a loaf of French bread, and the best Bordeaux in your cellar.

TENDERLOIN OF BEEF IN A GINGERED BRANDY-MUSTARD SAUCE

This elegant entree was served by Chef Phillip McGuire at the twentieth anniversary celebration of The Blue Strawbery. So many diners asked for the recipe that the restaurant printed copies. Yes, there is just one *r* in *Strawbery*. The restaurant is housed in a restored 1797 ship's chandlery overlooking the historical harbor in Portsmouth, New Hampshire. All food is freshly prepared for their dinner guests, who come by confirmed reservation only.

6 Servings
Marinate: 1 hour
Preparation Time: 10 minutes
Cooking Time: 1 hour

2 tbsp. shredded ginger
½ cup brandy
4 cloves garlic, crushed
freshly ground black
     pepper
salt
2 lb. beef tenderloin,
     trimmed of fat

1 tsp. butter
4 shallots, diced
4 cups sliced fresh
     mushrooms
½ cup beef stock
3 tbsp. Dijon mustard

1. Preheat oven to 450 degrees.

2. In a small bowl, combine ginger and brandy and let sit for one hour.

3. Rub 2 cloves of the garlic, pepper, and a small amount of salt on the outside of the beef. Roast in a 450-degree oven for about 30 minutes, or until just firm, not springy to the touch. Remove from the oven and pour the brandy and ginger over the meat. Carefully ignite the dish with a match held over the pan. When the flame goes out, cover the meat and let it rest while preparing sauce.

4. In a skillet, melt the butter, then add the shallots and remaining garlic. Sauté over high heat until they just start to brown, about 1 minute. Add mushrooms, stock, and mustard. Simmer for about 10 to 15 minutes, or until sauce is reduced by ⅔. Add the brandy-ginger mixture from the beef pan and simmer for 5 minutes more, or until slightly thickened.

5. Slice the beef onto a serving platter. Spoon the sauce over the beef and serve.

ONE SERVING: 455 Calories; 23.5 grams Fat (7.9 Saturated); 172 mg Cholesterol.

NOTE: A pork "loin" roast is not a tenderloin. Even some butchers seem to get confused. Pork tenderloin looks similar to a beef tenderloin — a rounded length of lean meat, weighing less than a pound. Ready to be sliced into medallions, roasted, or grilled, tenderloins are low in fat and a joy for any cook who treasures minimal preparation time.

NICE WITH: Corn bread made with the addition of ½ cup low-fat Monterey Jack cheese and a handful of chopped green onions.

CHICO'S CHILI

Another winner from Chef Marian Stapleton, who calls it "a chili for a summer night." It is the perfect entree for advance preparation and entertaining.

4 Servings
Preparation Time: 15 minutes
Cooking Time: 1 hour

cooking oil spray
1 lb. pork tenderloin, trimmed of fat and cut in ¼-inch cubes
1 medium onion, diced
3 cloves garlic, minced
1 30-oz. can crushed tomatoes, undrained
1 4-oz. can chopped mild green chili peppers
½ cup fresh corn kernels
½ tsp. ground cumin
1 tbsp. chili powder (or more to taste)
½ tsp. salt
4 small zucchini, quartered lengthwise and thinly sliced
chopped jalepeno peppers (optional garnish)
1 cup light sour cream or plain yogurt (optional)
chopped cilantro for garnish

1. Spray a large, heavy saucepan with oil. Over medium heat, sauté pork, onion, and garlic until pork is lightly browned, about 5 minutes.

2. Add tomatoes, green chilies, corn, cumin, chili powder, and salt to pork mixture. Bring to a boil, then reduce heat. Cover and simmer for 30 minutes.

3. Add zucchini. Cover and continuing cooking for about 15 minutes, or until pork is tender.

4. Serve in a bowl. Add chopped jalepeno peppers along with the milder green chilies, or pass them at the table along with any of the other optional garnishes.

ONE SERVING: 338 Calories; 13 grams Fat (4.8 Saturated); 76 mg Cholesterol.

VEAL MEDALLIONS WITH BRAISED ENDIVES AND BOILED POTATOES

Chef Georges Haidon has slashed the fat of the old days' sauce, making a blissfully light version. Annually for three decades, the Maisonette has received the rarified Mobil Five-Star ranking. On one such occasion, the Mobil officials said about the Cincinnati restaurant, "Every detail of food and service creates a warmth of ambience equal to its culinary excellence."

4 Servings
Preparation Time: 30 minutes
Cooking Time: 30 minutes

8 small Belgian endives, cut lengthwise
1 tsp. margarine, melted
1 tbsp. lemon juice
½ cup water
salt and pepper
24 balls of fresh potatoes (cut with melon ball cutter)

olive oil
8 2-oz. veal medallions, pounded thin
4 large tomatoes, peeled, seeded, and diced
4 tbsp. chopped shallots
4 tbsp. chopped fresh dill
4 tbsp. chopped fresh tarragon

1. Place the endives in a large skillet. Pour margarine and lemon juice over endives and season with a generous pinch of salt and pepper. Add ½ cup water. Simmer just until tender, about 15 to 20 minutes. Remove from heat. Do not drain.

2. Meanwhile, in a saucepan with boiling water, cook the potato balls just until a fork will pierce, about 10 minutes. Set aside.

3. Brush a skillet lightly with olive oil. Sauté veal until lightly brown and tender. Set aside and keep warm.

4. In a hot non-stick skillet, add tomatoes and shallots. Sauté briefly, adding some of the cooking liquid from the endives. Season with additional salt and pepper, if desired. Cook until slightly thick. Add dill and tarragon.

HEALTH TIP: Chef Haidon has eliminated salt from this recipe by relying on herbs and fresh lemon juice for the flavor. To restrict sodium in your diet, replace salt with lemon juice, fruit vinegars, grated fresh ginger, or chopped fresh garlic. Fresh chilies and spices also add their own distinctive boosts without a trace of sodium.

5. Drain endives and arrange 2 on each serving plate. Place 2 veal medallions on top. Spoon tomato sauce over veal. Arrange boiled potatoes around plate.

ONE SERVING: 253 Calories; 5.9 grams Fat (2.4 Saturated); 133 mg Cholesterol.

LAMB SPIRALS WITH PINE NUTS AND GARLIC

Need an inspiration to fire up the grill? Look no farther than this sizzling recipe—adapted from the one that Chef William Hufferd serves at the trendy DC3 in Santa Monica, California.

4 Servings
Preparation and Cooking Time: 45 minutes

4 4-oz. portions of boneless lean lamb, pounded to ¼-inch thickness
¼ cup minced roasted garlic

2 tbsp. toasted pine nuts
1 tbsp. olive oil
salt and freshly ground black pepper

1. Preheat grill.

2. Place lamb pieces flat on a cutting board. In a food processor or blender, mix garlic, pine nuts, and olive oil until smooth. Season with a pinch of salt and pepper, then spread evenly over lamb. Roll the lamb into 4 cylinders and tie with string to hold in shape. Sprinkle with salt and pepper.

3. Grill the lamb rolls to medium rare, about 4 to 5 minutes. Remove string and slice each lamb roll into 4 spirals.

ONE SERVING: 244 Calories; 4.6 grams Fat; 39 mg Cholesterol.

NOTE: See index for one method of roasting garlic.

NICE WITH: Roasted new potatoes and a salad tossed with a lemony vinaigrette and feta cheese.

IN A HURRY? Purchase pre-roasted garlic, or sauté ¼ cup minced garlic in a pan that has been sprayed with cooking oil.

PIRI-PIRI VINAIGRETTE
(For Grilled Steak)

Low-calorie excitement from Hamersley's Bistro. The heat level can be adjusted by altering the amount of red pepper.

Makes about ½ cup
Preparation Time: 1½ hours

¼ cup water
1 tbsp. dried crushed red
   pepper
¼ tsp. dried thyme,
   crumbled
2 tbsp. chopped shallots
6 cloves garlic, coarsely
   chopped

½ tsp. ground ginger
½ tsp. salt
¼ cup olive oil
¼ cup sherry wine
   vinegar or red wine
   vinegar

1. Bring first 3 ingredients to boil in small saucepan. Remove from heat and let stand for 30 minutes. Drain, reserving red pepper and thyme in pan. Mix in shallots, garlic, ginger, and salt. Transfer to a processor and blend until smooth.

2. Return blended mixture to saucepan. Add oil and vinegar and cook over medium-low heat just until hot. Cool completely.

3. Strain vinaigrette into a bowl, pressing on solids with the back of a spoon. Mix 1 teaspoon of the solids into vinaigrette; then discard remaining solids. Serve at room temperature.

PER SERVING (1 tbsp.): 68 Calories; 6.8 grams Fat; 0 mg Cholesterol.

HEALTH TIP: Which steak is the leanest? Here are the skinniest six according to saturated fat content (for three ounces of cooked meat):
   Tenderloin: 3.2 grams
   Top loin: 3.1 grams
   Top sirloin: 2.4 grams
   Round tip: 2.1 grams
   Eye of round: 1.5 grams
   Top round: 1.4 grams

MAKE AHEAD: This vinaigrette can be prepared up to a day in advance.

MAKE AHEAD: The compote can be prepared one day ahead of time. Cover and refrigerate, then bring to room temperature before serving.

GARLIC, LEMON, OLIVE, AND MINT COMPOTE
(For Pork or Lamb)

At Hamersley's Bistro in Boston, the menu changes with the seasons, but this richly spiced relish appears regularly, not only with meat—some days it tops fresh red snapper. It is delicious with just about anything!

Makes about 1¼ cups
Preparation Time: 20 minutes

1 cup dry white wine
½ cup water
3 cloves garlic, thinly sliced
¾ tsp. cumin seeds
¾ tsp. sugar
½ tsp. dried crushed red pepper
3 tbsp. extra virgin olive oil

⅓ cup thinly sliced red onion
3 tbsp. fresh lemon juice
6 oil-cured black olives, pitted, coarsely chopped
3⅛-inch-thick lemon slices, each cut into 8 wedges
1 tbsp. minced fresh mint leaves

1. In a heavy, medium-sized saucepan, combine first six ingredients and bring to a boil. Reduce heat and simmer for about 10 minutes, stirring occasionally, until mixture is reduced to ¾ cup. Pour mixture into a bowl and allow to cool.

2. Add all remaining ingredients and stir to combine. Season with salt and pepper.

PER SERVING (1 tbsp.): 49 Calories; 4.7 grams Fat; 0 mg Cholesterol.

CABERNET CASSIS SAUCE
(For Beef or Veal)

This is one of the remarkable creations of Gethin D. Thomas, the chef at Adirondack's in Denver, Colorado. Whether you choose to complement beef or veal with this rich, complex sauce, an important Cabernet Sauvignon would be the perfect accompaniment.

Makes 1½ cups
Preparation Time: 5 minutes
Cooking Time: 30 minutes

¾ cup Cabernet
   Sauvignon
¼ cup black currants
2 tbsp. cassis syrup
2 cups poultry or lamb
   stock
1 clove garlic, minced

2 fresh basil leaves,
   minced
1 tsp. unsalted butter,
   chilled
salt and freshly ground
   white pepper

1. In a small, heavy, non-aluminum saucepan, boil the wine with the black currants and cassis syrup over high heat until the liquid is reduced by ¾ to a thick syrup, about 5 to 7 minutes.

2. Add the stock and simmer over medium heat for 10 to 15 minutes, skimming the surface frequently, until the sauce is thick enough to coat the back of a spoon and is reduced to about 1½ cups. Add the garlic and basil and swirl in the butter until thoroughly incorporated.

3. Strain the sauce through a fine-mesh sieve; then return it to the pan to warm through gently. Season to taste with salt and pepper.

4. To keep the sauce warm, set the saucepan inside a bowl or larger pan of hot, but not boiling water.

PER SERVING (2 tbsp.): 23.8 Calories; 0.2 grams Fat; 1.4 mg Cholesterol.

VARIATION: *If you want to serve a Pinot Noir or a Bordeaux, substitute that wine for the Cabernet Sauvignon in the sauce. Likewise, you can also use red currants and red currant syrup in place of the black currants and cassis.*

HINT: *Be sure to buy a high quality cassis syrup, available in most wine and liquor shops or gourmet markets. Black currant liquors are not acceptable substitutes.*

Vegetables
and
Side Dishes

Vegetables and Side Dishes

Rice Primavera
Eggplant Creole
Lentil, Red Pepper, and Onion Sauté
Vegetable Sauté with Tuscan Spice Mix
Chef Johnny's Mardi Gras Vegetable Jambalaya
Broccoli-Pickled Eggplant Stir-Fry
Tomatoes Stuffed with Eggplant and Potato Purée
Oven-Baked Polenta
Vegetable Ragout
Roasted Vegetables Provençal
Zocalo Black Beans
Chinese Stir-Fried Broccoli or Zucchini
New-Way Risotto
Wild Rice Compote
Roasted Garlic
Pecan Brown Rice
Wild Rice Cakes

HEALTH TIP: Using long-grain brown rice in this recipe admirably boosts nutrition. It supplies three times the dietary fiber of white rice and more vitamins, minerals, and protein.

RICE PRIMAVERA

At Yuca in Miami, Chef Douglas Rodriguez makes this a complete meal by adding asparagus tips, mushroom caps, sliced beets, and fried onion rings.

4 Servings
Preparation Time: 30 minutes
Cooking Time: 15 minutes

2 tbsp. pure virgin olive oil
2 tbsp. minced garlic
¾ cup julienned red onion
¾ cup julienned leeks
¾ cup julienned carrots
¾ cup julienned zucchini
¾ cup julienned yellow squash
¾ cup julienned red pepper
½ cup fresh sweet green peas
½ cup sweet corn kernels
3 tbsp. sherry
3 tbsp. vegetable or chicken stock
salt and pepper to taste
6 cups cooked rice

1. Preheat oven to 250 degrees.

2. In a large skillet, heat olive oil. Add garlic, onion, leeks, carrots, zucchini, squash, pepper, peas, and corn. Sauté for 3 minutes, or until carrots are tender. Remove vegetables and deglaze pan with sherry. Add stock, and salt and pepper to taste. Add rice and mix well with vegetables.

3. Place in a baking dish and bake for 3 minutes in the preheated oven.

ONE SERVING: 268 Calories; 10.9 grams Fat (1.5 Saturated); 0 mg Cholesterol.

EGGPLANT CREOLE

With all the spice of Creole, this dish has zero cholesterol and barely a smidgen of oil. A member of the Fine Dining Hall of Fame, John Folse oversees the kitchen of Lafitte's Landing, which is housed in a restored Acadian cottage dating to 1797.

6 Servings
Total Preparation and Cooking Time: About 1 hour

1 large eggplant, cut into
    ½-inch cubes
¼ cup fresh lemon juice
1 tsp. corn oil margarine,
    softened
1 large onion, chopped
3 cloves garlic, minced
¼ cup white wine
1 small red bell pepper,
    finely chopped
4 tbsp. tomato paste
3 large tomatoes, cut into
    ½-inch cubes

2 tbsp. parsley, minced
1 bay leaf
½ tsp. thyme
¼ tsp. red pepper sauce
    (or to taste)
4 green onion tops, thinly
    sliced
1 cup coarsely crumbled
    French bread crumbs
salt and freshly ground
    pepper to taste

1. Preheat oven to 350 degrees.

2. Cook eggplant in boiling water until tender. Drain in colander. Place eggplant in a large bowl, add lemon juice, and toss well. Set aside.

3. In a large skillet, melt margarine, then sauté onion and garlic briefly. Add wine, and cook over low heat until wine evaporates completely and onions are tender.

4. Add red pepper and tomato paste; stir well and cook until peppers are soft. Add tomatoes; cook and stir until juices evaporate.

5. Add eggplant to the skillet mixture along with parsley, bay leaf, thyme, and red pepper sauce. Fold in green onion tops and bread crumbs. Add salt and pepper to taste.

HINT: Leftovers are great tossed with hot or cold pasta and freshly grated parmesan cheese!

MAKE AHEAD: May be made ahead through Step Five. Refrigerate and bring to room temperature before baking.

6. Place in an oven-proof dish and bake for 30 minutes at 350 degrees. Remove bay leaf and serve immediately. May also be served at room temperature.

ONE SERVING: 97.5 Calories; 1.7 grams Fat; 0 mg Cholesterol.

LENTIL, RED PEPPER, AND ONION SAUTE

This is a creamy side dish of onions, artichokes, and protein-packed lentils that would be great paired with chicken hot off the grill. The King Cole restaurant in Dayton, Ohio has earned the "Holiday Fine Dining Award" since 1955 and four stars from Mobil since 1978.

4 Servings
Preparation Time: 20 minutes (Using prepared lentils)

2 tbsp. olive oil
1 small red onion, diced
½ lb. small white
   mushrooms, sliced
2 cups cooked brown
   lentils
1 red pepper, diced

1 small jar marinated
   artichokes
2 tbsp. sherry wine
   vinegar
salt and pepper to taste
2 tomatoes, seeded and
   diced
2 tbsp. snipped chives

1. In a medium skillet, heat olive oil, then add onion and mushrooms. Sauté until lightly browned. Add the remaining ingredients and heat through.

ONE SERVING: 257 Calories; 11.0 grams Fat (2.2 Saturated); 0 mg Cholesterol.

A LITTLE LIGHTER?: To further reduce the fat in this recipe, you may wish to substitute quartered artichoke hearts that have been packed in water.

HEALTH TIP: When the nutrition awards are given out, lentils should take center stage. These button-shaped legumes are full of protein—over seventeen grams in just one cup—with nary a trace of cholesterol. Simmered in water or broth, they will be tender in about thirty-five minutes.

VEGETABLE SAUTE WITH TUSCAN SPICE MIX

Chef Steven Petusevsky says, "People should not be intimidated by healthy food choices." Apparently that's not a concern of diners at his natural food restaurant in Miami — ten thousand people dine at Unicorn Village every week!

4 Servings
Preparation Time: 15 minutes
Cooking Time: 10 minutes

1 tbsp. minced garlic
½ tsp. fennel seed
1 tsp. orange zest
    (minced orange peel)
¼ tsp. hot chili flakes
2 tbsp. minced basil
    leaves
½ tsp. dry oregano
2 tbsp. olive oil
4 stalks celery
1 medium red onion

1 medium eggplant,
    unpeeled
1 medium zucchini
1 large tomato
1½ heads escarole, well
    washed and patted
    dry
3 oz. cooked chick peas
3 oz. chopped black
    olives
cooked pasta or rice
    (optional)

1. Mix together the garlic, fennel, orange zest, chili flakes, basil, oregano, and 1 tablespoon olive oil. Combine well and set aside.

2. Chop celery, onion, eggplant, zucchini, and tomato into ½-inch dice. Cut escarole into similar small dice.

3. In a large, non-stick skillet, heat oil until hot. Add celery, red onion, and eggplant. Sauté for approximately 4 to 5 minutes, adding a few drops of water if required to soften ingredients. Add tomato, escarole, chick peas, olives, spice mix, and remaining tablespoon of olive oil. Continue sautéing until all vegetables are tender but still crunchy.

4. Serve over pasta or rice if desired.

ONE SERVING: 144 Calories; 6.1 grams Fat (0.8 Saturated); 0 mg Cholesterol.

HEALTH TIP: Substitute grated zests for salt in a low-sodium diet. Zest is the colored peel of citrus fruit that contains the tangy essential flavor oil of the fruit. Avoid the bitter white pulp beneath the skin.

NOTE: Creole seasoning and Piquant sauce can be found in the spice and flavoring section of specialty food markets.

HINT: Chef Johnny says, "One-day-old steamed rice is best for this recipe. For many dishes, home-made turkey stock is golden! I cover a turkey with water in a stockpot, simmer it until it is done, then remove and debone the meat. The stock that is rendered is fabulous for sautéing without oil, or as a flavor enhancer."

CHEF JOHNNY'S MARDI GRAS VEGETABLE JAMBALAYA

This is a signature dish of Chef Johnny "Jambalaya" Percle at Randolph Hall, the restaurant at Nottoway Plantation Home in White Castle, Louisiana. Notice how Percle uses an aromatic broth to cook the vegetables — no oil needed.

6 Servings
Preparation Time: 30 minutes
Cooking Time: 20 minutes

2 cups turkey stock
1 clove garlic, minced
½ tbsp. chopped fresh basil
½ tbsp. chopped fresh thyme
½ tbsp. chopped fresh oregano
1 tbsp. Creole seasoning
1 tbsp. Piquant sauce
2 carrots, cut into short, thin strips
1 green pepper, coarsely chopped
1 red pepper, coarsely chopped
1 golden pepper, coarsely chopped
1 stalk celery, coarsely chopped
1 large red onion, coarsely chopped
1 yellow squash, halved and thinly sliced
1 zucchini squash, halved and thinly sliced
12 young pea pods, cleaned and cut in 1-inch pieces
2 cups cooked rice
salt to taste

1. In a large skillet or stock pot, bring stock to a boil. Add garlic, herbs, Creole seasoning, and Piquant sauce. Add carrots, peppers, celery, onion, squash, and pea pods. Simmer for 5 to 10 minutes, or until vegetables are barely tender.

2. Add cooked rice. Stir and blend well. Cover and simmer for 3 to 5 minutes, or until liquid evaporates. Taste for seasoning, adding more Piquant sauce and salt to taste.

ONE SERVING: 192 Calories; 1.1 grams Fat; 0 mg Cholesterol.

BROCCOLI-PICKLED EGGPLANT STIR-FRY

At the Mansion on Turtle Creek, Dean Fearing serves these piquant vegetables with his *Swordfish and Toasted Rice Sauce.*

4 Servings
Preparation Time: 25 minutes
Marinate: at least 1 hour
Cooking Time: 10 minutes

½ cup plus 2 tbsp. sweetened rice wine vinegar
¼ cup sugar
2 tbsp. white wine vinegar
1 large eggplant, peeled and cut into large slices
1 shallot, peeled and finely chopped
1 clove garlic, peeled and finely chopped
2 tsp. finely grated fresh ginger
2 tbsp. chicken stock
¼ cup black soy sauce
1 tbsp. sesame oil
2 cups broccoli florets
½ cup julienned carrots

1. In a small bowl, combine ½ cup rice vinegar, sugar, and white wine vinegar. Mix thoroughly to dissolve sugar. Pour over eggplant and allow to marinate for at least 1 hour.

2. In a small bowl, combine shallot, garlic, ginger, chicken stock, soy sauce, and remaining 2 tablespoons rice vinegar. Set aside.

3. Pour eggplant slices into a strainer and let stand for 10 minutes or until all the liquid has drained off.

4. In a large sauté pan, heat sesame oil over high heat. Immediately add broccoli and carrots. Stir-fry for 1 minute. Add well-drained eggplant and stir-fry for another 2 minutes, allowing eggplant to brown as much as possible.

5. Add soy sauce mixture, a tablespoon at a time, until vegetables are well seasoned (there should be no standing liquid in the pan). Remove and serve immediately.

ONE SERVING: 150 Calories; 5.1 grams Fat (0.7 Saturated); 0 mg Cholesterol.

NOTE: Sweetened rice wine vinegar can be found in the Asian section of most specialty food markets. Black soy sauce has had molasses added. The more common variety is referred to as "dark" soy sauce.

HEALTH TIP: Broccoli, along with its relatives of the Brassica genus—such as cabbage and brussel spouts—have been shown to have cancer-preventing properties.

NICE WITH: Need a speedy side dish? Run the end of the butter stick along steamed asparagus spears for just a kiss of flavor. Top with thin twists of lemon.

TOMATOES STUFFED WITH EGGPLANT AND POTATO PUREE

This is one of the "20th Anniversary Favorite Recipes" from The Blue Strawbery in Portsmouth, New Hampshire.

6 Servings
Preparation Time: 20 minutes
Cooking Time: 20 minutes

1 cup chicken stock, white wine, or water
1 medium eggplant, peeled and chopped into ¼-inch cubes
2 medium potatoes, peeled and chopped into ¼-inch cubes
1 clove garlic, chopped
1 small onion, chopped
¼ cup plus 2 tbsp. grated parmesan cheese
2 tbsp. chopped chives or scallions
salt and pepper
6 medium tomatoes

1. Preheat oven to 400 degrees.

2. In a covered pan, combine stock (or wine or water), eggplant, and potatoes. Steam until the vegetables are soft, about 5 to 7 minutes. Do not drain.

3. Place mixture in a food processor or blender along with the garlic, onion, ¼ cup parmesan cheese, and chives (or scallions). Purée until smooth. Add salt and pepper to taste.

4. Cut a thin slice from the bottom of each tomato. Core from the stem end, removing about ½ of the tomato pulp. Stuff tomatoes with potato and eggplant mixture. Top with remaining 2 tablespoons parmesan cheese.

5. Place in a baking dish and bake in a 400-degree oven for about 20 minutes, or until brown on top and the tomato skin just starts to split. Serve immediately.

ONE SERVING: 103 Calories; 2.6 grams Fat; 5 mg Cholesterol.

OVEN-BAKED POLENTA

Bravo to Chef Steven Hunn who found a way for us to enjoy creamy, cheesy polenta—with an intriguing hint of basil—without all the stirring!

8 Servings
Preparation Time: 5 minutes
Cooking Time: 1 hour

3½ cups chicken stock
½ cup cornmeal
salt and freshly ground
    pepper

½ tbsp. chopped fresh
    basil
¼ cup freshly shredded
    romano cheese
2 tbsp. butter

1. Preheat oven to 325 degrees.

2. In a large saucepan, bring stock to a boil and gradually add the cornmeal in a thin stream, whisking constantly until slightly thickened. Add salt and pepper to taste.

3. Transfer the mixture to a shallow pan, cover with foil, and place in a larger pan filled with water to the level of the cornmeal.

4. Bake in a 325-degree oven for 45 minutes. Remove from oven and stir in romano cheese and basil. Serve immediately or chill, cut into shapes, and reheat in a microwave.

ONE SERVING: 147 Calories; 7.4 grams Fat (4.3 Saturated); 16 mg Cholesterol.

VARIATION: Try adding freshly grated corn to the mixture before baking. Skim milk can be substituted for part of the broth.

VEGETABLE RAGOUT

Stephan Pyles creates a bouquet of intense flavors in this vegetable-herb stew. In French, an all-vegetable ragout is known as *ragout a la printanière*, a stew for springtime. At Routh Street Cafe in Dallas, Chef Stephan Pyles was the first Texan named to Who's Who of Cooking in America.

6 Main Dish Servings
Preparation and Cooking Time: 1 hour

HEALTH TIP: Mother was right; you should eat your vegetables. All health organizations agree that eating higher proportions of vegetables cuts down on total fat and calorie consumption, reduces the risk of heart disease, and boosts intake of beta carotene, vitamin C, fiber, and other nutrients.

5 medium tomatoes
4 tbsp. olive oil
½ cup peeled eggplant, cut into ¼-inch cubes
½ cup onions, cut into ¼-inch cubes
½ cup zucchini, cut into ¼-inch cubes
2 tbsp. garlic, finely minced
1 tbsp. chopped fresh thyme,
1 tbsp. chopped fresh oregano
2 tbsp. tomato paste
¼ cup fresh basil, chopped
¼ cup parsley, chopped
salt and pepper to taste

1. Fill a large saucepan with water to ¾ full and bring to a boil. Have a large bowl of ice water handy. With a sharp knife, core the top of each tomato and cut a small X through the skin on the bottom. Place the tomatoes in the boiling water for approximately 1 minute, or until skin begins to pull away from meat. Plunge tomatoes into ice water and cool for 1 minute. Skin should slip off tomatoes easily. Remove skin and slice tomatoes in half. Squeeze to remove seeds. Cut tomato into ¼-inch cubes and place in a strainer over a bowl.

2. In a large skillet, heat 2 tablespoons of the olive oil until lightly smoking, add the eggplant, and sauté for 5 minutes. (Eggplant should be translucent.) Place eggplant in a colander and weigh down with a plate to remove the bitter juices. Heat the remaining 2 tablespoons olive oil until lightly smoking, then add the onion and zucchini. Sauté for 2 minutes, then add the garlic, thyme, oregano, tomato paste, and tomatoes. Cook until all liquid has evaporated, about 10 to 15 minutes. Add basil, parsley, and eggplant and continue cooking for 2 minutes. Season with salt and freshly ground pepper.

ONE SERVING: 276.4 Calories; 11.2 grams Fat (1.0 Saturated); 0 mg Cholesterol.

ROASTED VEGETABLES PROVENÇAL

Chef Philippe Jeanty, a native of Champagne, France, relocated to the kitchen of the famous champagne winery, Domaine Chandon, in Napa Valley, California. This is an adaptation of his classic ratatouille made new with reduced-fat oven roasting rather than the usual sautéing. At Domaine Chandon, menus are planned to highlight the wealth of fresh ingredients available in California, as well as the versatility of sparkling wine with food. Not surprisingly, the restaurant at Domaine Chandon boasts the highest per customer consumption of sparkling wine in the United States—2 glasses per patron.

8 Servings
Preparation Time: 30 minutes
Cooking Time: 25 minutes

1 medium acorn,
    butternut, or
    pumpkin squash
4 tomatoes
4 medium zucchini
6 Japanese eggplant or
    1 small eggplant

3 tbsp. olive oil
3 tbsp. herbes de
    Provence or a mixture
    of fresh herbs
salt and pepper
fresh basil leaves for
    garnish

1. Preheat oven to 500 degrees.

2. Peel acorn squash, cut in half and cut in half again. Scrape out seeds and fiber; then cut into ⅛-inch-thick slices.

3. Cut tomatoes across, then cut slices in half. Cut off both ends of zucchini, then cut in half lengthwise and julienne. Cut unpeeled eggplant in thin diagonal slices.

4. Coat bottom and sides of a 9 x 12 baking dish with 1 tablespoon olive oil. Add vegetables, alternating layers and sprinkling herbs, the remaining 2 tablespoons of olive oil, and salt and pepper on each layer.

5. Bake at 500 degrees for 12 minutes. Lower heat to 400 degrees and bake for another 5 to 6 minutes, just until vegetables are tender.

HINT: Herbes de Provence is a spice mix that can be found in specialty food markets. If unavailable, substitute any combination of herbs, but basil, fennel, and oregano should be considered for capturing the mood of Chef Jeanty's dish.

6. Serve hot or at room temperature, garnished with fresh basil leaves.

ONE SERVING: 149 Calories; 6.1 grams Fat (1.1 Saturated); 0 mg Cholesterol.

ZOCALO BLACK BEANS

In Mexico, a *zocalo* is a meeting place. In Philadelphia, the vibrant flavors of Mexican food are recreated by Chef Lou Sackett in her restaurant of the same name. Zocalo was twice the winner of the "Best of Philly" award for Mexican food. Here's a robust side dish that goes perfectly with her *Enchiladas Verdes*.

Makes about 2 quarts
Preparation Time: 4 to 6 hours to soak beans
Cooking Time: 2 hours

½ lb. black turtle beans
1 cup chopped white onion
¼ cup minced fresh garlic
1 tbsp. minced serrano chile
2 tbsp. minced chiles chipotles en adobo
1 cup peeled, seeded, chopped tomato
kosher salt to taste
¼ cup chopped cilantro

1. Pick over beans and rinse well. Soak for 4 to 6 hours covered with twice as much water as there are beans in a non-aluminum pan.

2. Drain beans and place in a saucepan with water to cover. Bring to a simmer and skim off foam.

3. Add onion, garlic, serranos, and chipotles. Simmer gently, partially covered, for 1 to 1½ hours, adding water as necessary until beans are just tender.

4. Add tomato, salt, and cilantro. Simmer 15 to 20 minutes more.

ONE SERVING (8 oz.): 171 Calories; 0.8 grams Fat (0.2 Saturated); 0 mg Cholesterol.

NOTE: Chiles chipotles en adobo are canned smoked jalepeno peppers. They can be found in Mexican specialty food markets or ordered from catalogues that feature southwestern ingredients.

HEALTH TIP: For generations, Mexican cooks have based their diet on recommended nutritional guidelines. High-fiber grains and legumes are the energy-giving foundation of this ancient cuisine. At Zocalo, you can enjoy the traditional Mexican trio of complex carbohydrates—hot corn tortillas, seasoned rice, and black beans.

CHINESE STIR-FRIED BROCCOLI OR ZUCCHINI

Aboard the cruise ship, *Golden Odyssey*, cooking expert Lucy Chu shows her students how to prepare perfectly tender broccoli and zucchini.

Broccoli:

6 Servings

1 bunch broccoli
2 qt. water

2 tbsp. cooking oil
½ tsp. salt
¼ tsp. sugar

1. Bring water to a boil. Cut the stems from the broccoli head and boil the stems for 2 minutes. Rinse in cold water, then peel off the stringy skin. Slice stems into rounds.

2. Cut the florets into uniform size, about 1½ x ½ inch. Place into the boiling water and boil for 1 minute. Rinse in cold water and drain.

3. In a wok over high heat, stir-fry broccoli in the oil for about 3 minutes. Add salt and sugar and stir to mix.

ONE SERVING (½ cup): 62.6 Calories; 4.7 grams Fat: 0 mg Cholesterol.

Zucchini:

4 Servings

5 cups peeled zucchini
    slices, cut ¼ inch
    thick

2 tbsp. cooking oil
1 tsp. salt
½ tsp. sugar

1. In a wok over high heat, stir-fry zucchini in the oil for about 3 minutes. Season with salt and sugar. May be served at room temperature.

ONE SERVING (½ cup): 53.6 Calories; 6.4 grams Fat; 0 mg Cholesterol.

HINT: Lucy says, "Broccoli will not be a delicately textured green vegetable unless you peel off the stringy skin from the stems." Lucy peels the zucchini, but you may prefer to leave the skin on. Cooking time will be the same. The salt is optional for those on a low-sodium diet.

NEW-WAY RISOTTO

HEALTH TIP: *Although it is possible to buy reduced-fat and low-sodium broth, the tastiest, healthiest broth comes from the soup pot in your own kitchen. To prepare a simple but delicious defatted chicken stock, combine two pounds of chicken, two cups of chopped aromatic vegetables (such as onion, garlic, and carrots), and the herbs of your choice; then cover with water and simmer for at least one hour. Strain the broth, refrigerate it overnight, then skim the congealed fat from the surface. Pour the broth into containers of convenient size, and freeze for later use.*

"Classic risotto calls for lots of butter, but that's not what makes it creamy," says Chef Emile Mooser. "The secret is in the stirring. The more you stir, the more the rice grains rub against each other and brush off the outer layer of starch." Chef Mooser cut butter out of his own diet nine years ago and trimmed down the high-fat French dishes on the menu at Emile's in San Jose, California. He says, "I know all the reasons why butter is used in classic dishes, so I can always find a good substitute."

4 Servings
Preparation Time: 10 minutes
Cooking Time: 50 minutes

3 to 4 cups defatted stock
2 tsp. olive oil
1 carrot, finely diced
1 parsnip, finely diced

1½ cups Arborio or
short-grain rice
parmesan cheese
(optional)

1. In a saucepan, bring the stock to a boil. Reduce the heat to low and keep warm.

2. In another large, heavy-bottomed saucepan over medium-low heat, combine oil, carrot, and parsnip. Sauté until tender, about 10 minutes. Add the rice.

3. Raise the heat to medium. Add 1 cup of the stock and stir well. Cover the pan and cook, stirring every few minutes, until the stock has been absorbed. Add another cup of stock and repeat the process. Continue adding as much of the remaining stock as necessary to produce rice that is very creamy and thick, but still a bit firm to the bite, at least 30 minutes.

ONE SERVING: 140 Calories; 4.7 grams Fat (.8 Saturated); 0 mg Cholesterol.

WILD RICE COMPOTE

HEALTH TIP: Wild rice is very high in fiber and belongs in any gourmet's low-fat diet.

Chef Rick Cunningham invented this artful combination of tangy fruit and ham simmered with nutty brown rice. He serves it alongside his *Cornish Game Hen with Orange Apricot Sauce* at Ivy's restaurant in San Francisco.

6 Servings
Preparation Time: 45 minutes
Cooking Time: 35 to 45 minutes

1½ cups wild rice, soaked in water ½ hour and drained
5 cups water
1 tsp. salt
2 tsp. olive oil
⅓ cup lean diced ham (optional)

1 cup chopped leeks, white part only
⅓ cup chopped dried fruit (apricots, peaches, etc.)
½ cup chicken stock
½ to 1 cup plain low-fat yogurt
salt and pepper to taste

1. After soaking rice, combine with water and salt. Bring to a boil, reduce heat, cover, and simmer for about 35 to 40 minutes, until rice is tender and most of the grains have split slightly. Drain excess liquid and fluff with a fork.

2. Meanwhile, in a large sauté pan, heat olive oil. Add ham, leeks, and dried fruit and sauté until leeks are tender.

3. Add chicken stock and wild rice and cook until the liquid disappears, 2 to 3 minutes.

4. Add yogurt. Mix well and season with salt and pepper to taste.

ONE SERVING (With ham): 284 Calories; 2.7 grams Fat; 16 mg Cholesterol.

ROASTED GARLIC

VARIATION: Chef Cowman suggests experimenting with herbs other than thyme.

At the Upperline restaurant in New Orleans, Chef Tom Cowman serves his sweet garlic with roasted new potatoes. Try it also as an appetizer, spread on French bread. The *Times-Picayune* restaurant critic wrote, "New Orleans' reputation as a restaurant town is secure as long as chefs of Tom Cowman's caliber are shaking the sauté pans and firing up the grills!"

10 Servings
Preparation Time: 10 minutes
Cooking Time: 45 minutes

10 whole unpeeled heads garlic	**1 tbsp. kosher salt**
2 tbsp. olive oil	**½ tsp. freshly ground black pepper**
1 tbsp. chopped fresh thyme	

1. Preheat oven to 350 degrees.

2. Slice off and discard the top third of the garlic heads. Remove outer layers of skin.

3. In a 11 x 7-inch baking pan, thoroughly combine remaining ingredients. Place garlic cut-side down in pan. Roast garlic for 35 to 45 minutes in a 350-degree oven, or until cloves are soft and the cut edges are slightly caramelized.

4. To serve, press cloves lightly to squeeze out soft garlic.

ONE SERVING: 114 Calories; 7.5 grams Fat (.8 Saturated); 0 mg Cholesterol.

PECAN BROWN RICE

According to diners at The Tree Top House in Berkley, West Virginia, this is the perfect accompaniment to *Grilled Lobster and Scallop Kebobs*.

6 Servings
Preparation Time: 10 minutes
Cooking Time: 1 hour

cooking oil spray	**½ tsp. dried whole thyme**
½ cup finely chopped green onion	**⅛ tsp. pepper**
1½ cup water	**1 cup brown rice**
1½ tsp. instant chicken bouillon	**¼ cup toasted chopped pecans**
	2 tbsp. chopped parsley

HEALTH TIP: You get more for your nutritional dollar when you bypass refined white rice for nutty-flavored brown rice. It is the only form of rice that contains fiber-rich bran and vitamin E. If you are not yet accustomed to the taste, try mixing it with white rice.

1. Coat a large, oven-proof covered saucepan with cooking oil spray. Heat over medium heat and add onion. Sauté until tender. Add water, bouillon, thyme, and pepper. Bring to a boil, add rice, and stir.

2. Cover pan and bake in a 350-degree oven for 50 minutes or until the liquid is absorbed. Stir in pecans and chopped parsley and serve.

ONE SERVING: 110 Calories; 3.8 grams Fat (0.4 Saturated); 0 mg Cholesterol.

WILD RICE CAKES

Chef Steven Hunn has created the perfect side dish for his *Roast Pork Tenderloin with Lemon Pear Chutney*. The nutty flavor also makes these rice cakes a perfect companion to poultry dishes.

4 Servings
Preparation Time: 20 minutes (using prepared wild rice)

1½ tbsp. butter or margarine	salt and pepper to taste
½ cup diced red, green, and yellow peppers	2 egg whites
2 cups cooked wild rice	1 tsp. minced fresh herbs (thyme, marjoram, or savory)
½ cup low-fat milk	1 cup bread crumbs

1. In a skillet, heat 1 tablespoon butter and sauté the peppers. Add rice, milk, salt, and pepper and mix thoroughly. Remove from heat. When the mixture is cool enough to handle, stir in the egg whites, herbs, and ½ cup of the bread crumbs. (It may be necessary to add some or all of the remaining bread crumbs.) Shape into oval cakes.

2. In a heavy, non-stick skillet, heat the remaining ½ tablespoon butter and sauté the rice cakes until they are heated through and crispy.

ONE SERVING: 174 Calories; 4.9 grams Fat (2.7 Saturated); 10 mg Cholesterol.

HINT: Pecans can be quickly toasted by placing them on a pan in a small toaster oven. Use the toast setting with the temperature set at 325 degrees. They can also be toasted by tossing and stirring them in a skillet over medium heat.

HEALTH TIP: Chef Hunn's original recipe used eggs and heavy cream, but he comments, "These ingredients are just used as binders. You can substitute cholesterol-free egg whites and low-fat milk and not miss the cream at all. The flavor is still marvelous!"

Desserts

Desserts

Roasted Pears with Bitter Chocolate Sorbet
Orange Cloud Cakes with Boysenberry Sauce
Floating Island on Strawberry Purée with Kiwi
Apricot Soufflé with Brandy Sauce
Christmas Italian Rice Pudding
Chocolate Madeleines
Strawberry Grapefruit Soufflé
Hawaiian Sorbet
Papaya-Serrano Chile Ice
Raspberry Mousse
Mixed Berry and Granola Crisp
Pears Poached in White Wine with Raspberry Sauce
Mango Mousse

ROASTED PEARS WITH BITTER CHOCOLATE SORBET

"You eat with all your senses," says Chef Mooser of Emile's in San Jose. "In a satisfying dessert, taste, texture, temperature, appearance, and aroma are all important."

4 Servings
Preparation Time: 1 hour (plus freezing time)

1¾ cups skim milk
½ cup fruit concentrate
⅓ cup cocoa
½ vanilla bean, halved
    lengthwise

2 tbsp. evaporated skim
    milk
2 Bosc pears

1. In a 2-quart saucepan over medium heat, bring the skim milk almost to a boil. Add the fruit concentrate, cocoa, and vanilla bean. Let steep for 10 minutes. Strain into a large bowl, add the evaporated milk, and allow to cool.

2. Transfer to an ice cream maker and freeze according to the manufacturer's directions.

3. About 30 minutes before serving, halve and core the pears. Place, cut side down, on a non-stick baking sheet. Bake at 375 degrees until tender and lightly caramelized on the underside, about 20 minutes.

4. To make pear fans, slice the pears into thin strips, starting at the bottom of each pear and stopping just short of the stem end. Place on dessert plates and fan out slices. Serve immediately with the sorbet.

ONE SERVING: 257 Calories; 1.5 grams Fat; 2 mg Cholesterol.

ORANGE CLOUD CAKES WITH BOYSENBERRY SAUCE

Chef Louis Chevot says that his guests at the Topnotch Resort and Spa in Stowe, Vermont are often incredulous of the fact that desserts such as this are actually low in calories.

6 Servings
Preparation Time: 35 minutes
Baking Time: 20 minutes

2 cups frozen
    boysenberries,
    thawed, undrained
3 tbsp. sugar
solid vegetable
    shortening
¼ cup whole wheat flour
¼ cup all purpose flour
½ tsp. baking powder
¼ tsp. baking soda
⅛ tsp. salt

1 egg yolk
2 tbsp. nonfat milk
2 tbsp. vegetable oil
1½ tsp. grated orange
    peel
½ tsp. vanilla extract
¼ vanilla bean, split
    lengthwise (optional)
3 egg whites
1½ tsp. powdered sugar

1. Preheat oven to 350 degrees.

2. In a food processor, process berries and 1 tablespoon of sugar until puréed. Strain to remove seeds.

3. Grease six ⅔-cup custard cups or soufflé dishes with solid vegetable shortening. In a medium bowl, sift flours, sugar, baking powder, baking soda, and salt. In a small bowl, whisk egg yolk, milk, vegetable oil, orange peel, and vanilla extract. Scrape seeds from vanilla bean into egg yolk mixture. Add to dry ingredients and mix until just combined.

4. Using an electric mixer, beat egg whites with powdered sugar until stiff but not dry. Fold into batter. Divide batter among prepared cups. Bake in a 350-degree oven until golden brown and tester inserted into centers comes out clean, about 20 minutes.

VARIATION: Blueberries may be substituted for the boysenberries.

HEALTH TIP: Like all fruits, boysenberries with their natural sweetness make the perfect healthful snack or dessert. To benefit from the extra vitamins and fiber, eat or prepare washed fruit with the peel intact whenever possible.

5. Using a small sharp knife, cut between cakes and cups to loosen. Transfer cakes to serving plate and serve with sauce.

ONE SERVING: 186 Calories; 1.6 grams Fat; 54 mg Cholesterol.

NOTE: The kiwi fruit comes from New Zealand with instructions to hold the kiwi between the thumb and forefinger to see if it is ripe. If it is soft, it is ready to eat. Cut in half lengthwise and lift out flesh with a small spoon, or peel and slice across. The fruit is completely edible—even the brown skin can either be eaten or used as a napkin to keep the fingers clean."

FLOATING ISLAND ON STRAWBERRY PUREE WITH KIWI FRUIT

This, from Chef Georges Haidon, is a new version of a classic dish the French call *Oeufs a la Neige* or "Snowy Eggs." Meringue "eggs" float on red berry sauce—a just dessert after a sumptuous meal at the Maisonette.

4 Servings
Preparation Time: 45 minutes

4 egg whites
4 packs artificial
sweetener

32 strawberries, puréed
4 small kiwi, peeled and
sliced

1. Beat egg whites. When they start to turn white, add the sweetener. Beat until very stiff.

2. Bring a skillet of water to boil. Reduce heat to simmer. Spoon the egg white into the simmering water, forming them into 4 egg shapes. Cook for 10 minutes, turning to cook evenly. Do not allow the water to boil. When cooked, remove the "eggs" carefully with a slotted spoon, dry on towel and let cool.

3. Spread strawberry purée on a plate. Place a meringue "egg" in the center. Arrange kiwi slices to decorate the plate.

ONE SERVING: 84 Calories; 0.6 grams Fat; 0 mg Cholesterol.

APRICOT SOUFFLE WITH BRANDY SAUCE

MAKE AHEAD: The soufflé can be prepared through Step 3 and allowed to sit at room temperature for up to one hour before baking. The sauce may be may ahead and reheated just before serving.

Well-known Napa Valley chef Sally Schmitt is unsurpassed in imaginative food styling. Sample her cloudlike soufflé which is often the finale to an unforgettable meal at The French Laundry in Yountville, California.

4 Servings
Preparation Time: 1 hour
Baking Time: 30 minutes

1 cup dried apricots
2 cups water
⅓ cup brown sugar
¼ cup plus 4 tbsp. brandy

6 egg whites
⅓ cup plus ½ cup sugar
1 tbsp. flour
zest and juice of ½ lemon
2 tbsp. butter

1. Preheat oven to 350 degrees.

2. Stack and slice the apricots into a fine shred with a sharp knife. Place in a small, heavy-bottomed saucepan with 1 cup of water. Bring to a boil, lower heat, and allow to sit for 15 minutes. (The apricots should become quite soft.) Add brown sugar and brandy. Stir vigorously to a rough purée and set aside to cool.

3. Beat egg whites until just stiff, being careful not to over-beat. Gradually add ⅓ cup sugar. Fold a little egg white mixture into the apricot purée to lighten it; then fold the apricot mixture into the remaining egg whites. (The mixture need not be smooth, but there should be no streaks of egg white left.)

4. Butter and sugar a 1½-quart (or 2-quart) soufflé dish. Pour the mixture into dish and collar if necessary. Bake for 30 minutes in a 350-degree oven, or until the soufflé is puffed high and well-browned, but is not too shaky.

5. While the soufflé is baking, combine the ½ cup of sugar and flour in a large saucepan with high sides. Mix well, then

stir in the remaining cup of water. Let boil for about 5 minutes to cook the flour. Whisk in the lemon zest, lemon juice, brandy, and butter. When baked, the soufflé should be served immediately with the brandy sauce.

ONE SERVING: 308 Calories; 11.7 grams Fat (7.2 Saturated); 31 mg Cholesterol.

CHRISTMAS ITALIAN RICE PUDDING

Here's a healthy holiday gift for busy cooks. There's no need to stand over a hot stove—the ingredients go into the oven and come out a creamy rich dessert. At the Barrows House in Dorset, Vermont, this pudding is topped with cinnamon or sprinkles of Christmas colored sugar.

4 Servings
Preparation Time: 8 minutes
Cooking Time: About 2 hours

1 tbsp. vegetable oil
2 cups skim milk
¼ cup risotto (Italian short grain rice)
¼ cup sugar
½ vanilla bean or ½ tsp. vanilla extract
¼ cup dried black currants
cinnamon or colored sugars (optional garnish)

1. Preheat oven to 275 degrees.

2. Oil an 8½ x 4½-inch loaf pan. Add all ingredients to pan. Place in 275-degree oven and bake for approximately 2 ½ hours or until rice is cooked and liquid is absorbed. Stir every 15 to 20 minutes. (It may be necessary to add more milk if pudding gets too thick.)

3. Serve hot or chilled. Decorate with cinnamon or Christmas-colored sugars, if desired.

ONE SERVING: 253 Calories; 0.4 grams Fat; 2 mg Cholesterol.

HINT: In place of fat-laden whipping cream or whipped topping mixes, you can whip evaporated skimmed milk. To prepare, chill a mixing bowl, beaters of an electric mixer, and evaporated skimmed milk in the freezer for thirty minutes. Remove and beat milk on high speed until soft peaks form. Use as a topping for fresh fruit and angel food cake.

CHOCOLATE MADELEINES

Even chocoholics can have their healthy desserts with these light-as-a-feather French tea cakes from Chef Ronald Hook at the Doral Saturnia International Spa Resort.

Makes 30
Preparation Time: 30 minutes
Cooking Time: 15 minutes

5 oz. semi-sweet
   chocolate
3 oz. two percent milk
2 tbsp. unsalted butter
1 cup sugar
3 medium eggs
1 cup whole wheat cake
   flour

1 cup unbleached white
   flour
2 tsp. baking soda
1½ cups extra strong
   coffee, chilled
½ cup Madeira wine
spray cooking oil

1. Preheat oven to 350 degrees.

2. In a microwave or double boiler, heat chocolate with milk, just until the chocolate is melted. Set aside.

3. In a mixer, cream butter and sugar together. Add the eggs, one at a time, to the sugar, beating after each addition.

4. In a medium bowl, combine the two flours and the baking soda. Do not sift. In another bowl, combine the chilled coffee and wine.

5. Add flours and coffee mixture to the butter-sugar mixture in the mixer, alternating ⅓ at a time until well mixed.

6. Spray madeleine pan lightly with spray cooking oil. Fill each with ¾ ounce of the batter. Bake at 350 degrees for 10 to 15 minutes.

ONE SERVING (Two madeleines): 90 Calories; 3.0 grams Fat; 37 mg Cholesterol.

The New Larousse Gastronomique *tells us that madeleines—small cakes made of butter, flour, eggs, and sugar—may have been invented in the seventeenth century and brought into fashion at Versailles. The recipe for madeleines remained a secret for a very long time and was finally sold for "a very large sum" to the pastry makers of Commercy, France, who made this great delicacy one of the finest gastronomic specialties of their town.*

NOTE: This may also be baked in a bundt pan or a 9 x 11-inch cake pan. Bake for about thirty-five minutes. This batter is too thin for spring mold pans.

STRAWBERRY GRAPEFRUIT SOUFFLE

Palate-pleasing freshness comes in the form of a puffy soufflé of baked fruit at Fio's restaurant in St. Louis, Missouri.

4 Servings
Preparation Time: 25 minutes
Baking Time: 20-25 minutes

4 tbsp. grapefruit juice
¼ cup grapefruit sections, in bite-sized pieces
8 tbsp. puréed strawberries
4 tbsp. sliced fresh strawberries
8 egg whites

1 tbsp. flour
4 tsp. Grand Marnier
4 tbsp. fructose (available at health food stores)
1 tbsp. chopped fresh mint
whole mint leaves for garnish

1. Preheat oven to 400 degrees.

2. In a large bowl, combine 3 tablespoons grapefruit juice, grapefruit sections, 4 tablespoons puréed strawberries, 4 egg whites, flour, Grand Marnier, and fructose.

3. Beat remaining 4 egg whites to a soft peak and fold into the fruit mixture. Pour into a lightly greased 1-quart soufflé dish. Bake at 400 degrees until firm, about 20 to 25 minutes. Serve immediately with a sauce made by combining the remaining strawberry purée and grapefruit juice with the chopped mint. Garnish with mint leaves.

ONE SERVING: 126 Calories; 0.2 grams Fat; 0 mg Cholesterol.

HAWAIIAN SORBET

Chef Fio Antognini oversees a light menu at Fio's in St. Louis and conducts cooking school classes on the art of preparing gourmet low-calorie meals.

4 Servings
Preparation Time: 20 minutes (plus freezing time)

2 large ripe mangoes,
   peeled and seeded
1 large ripe banana,
   peeled
½ tsp. fresh mint,
   chopped

1 tbsp. orange juice
2 egg whites
1½ tbsp. fructose
seasonal berries for
   garnish

1. Cut mangoes and banana into chunks. In a blender, blend the two fruits with the chopped mint and orange juice.

2. Whip egg whites until stiff and fold into fruit mixture. Pour into ice cream maker (or ice trays) and freeze.

3. Serve in scoops garnished with berries.

ONE SERVING: 169 Calories; 0.7 grams Fat; 0 mg Cholesterol.

NICE WITH: This is ideal with any menu featuring Cuban, Spanish, Mexican, or Caribbean fare. Serve it either as a refreshing pause between courses or as a light dessert.

HEALTH TIP: Use fresh fruit and fruit juices whenever possible. If not available, look for unsweetened frozen fruit or frozen fruit juice concentrate.

PAPAYA-SERRANO CHILE ICE

When has 89 calories ever tasted so devilish? This refresher of sweet and heat is another sophisticated mix of southwestern ingredients from Routh Street Cafe in Dallas, Texas.

4 Servings
Preparation Time: 10 minutes
Chilling Time: At least 3 hours

2 cups peeled and cubed
   papayas
¼ cup orange juice
4 tsp. lime juice

¼ cup sugar dissolved in
   2 tbsp. hot water
1 serrano chile, seeded
   and finely diced

HINT: Serrano chiles look a bit like smaller, more pointed jalapenos, and are much hotter. This follows the general rule—the smaller the pepper the hotter the fire.

HEALTH TIP: Fruits contain at least ten times— often up to fifty times— the amount of energy-providing carbohydrates as do fats.

1. Place papaya cubes in a blender with orange juice, lime juice, sugar-water mixture, and chilies. Purée until smooth, about 1 minute.

2. Pour mixture into small mixing bowl and place in freezer for 1 hour. Remove and whisk vigorously, then return to freezer for at least 2 hours.

3. Serve in stemmed glasses.

ONE SERVING: 89 Calories; 0.1 grams Fat ; 0 mg Cholesterol.

RASPBERRY MOUSSE

Start with a pint of raspberries, and in ten minutes you'll have a dreamy swirl of a dessert—for an amazingly scant thirty-two calories and 0.2 grams of fat. Credit for this recipe goes to Chef Jean-Marie Lacroix, who serves it at The Four Seasons in Philadelphia.

4 Servings
Preparation Time: 10 minutes

1 pint raspberries　　　**4 oz. sugar substitute**
juice of ½ lemon　　　**3 egg whites**

1. Purée the raspberries, then add the lemon juice. Beat the egg whites until a firm consistency is reached. Slowly add sugar substitute, then carefully fold in the egg whites.

2. Spoon into glasses and serve immediately.

ONE SERVING: 32 Calories; 0.2 grams Fat; 0 mg Cholesterol.

MIXED BERRY AND
GRANOLA CRISP

Granola glitz is served at Unicorn Village in Miami, Florida, where everything Chef Steven Petusevsky offers at this natural food restaurant is prepared from scratch.

4 Servings
Preparation Time: 15 minutes
Cooking Time: 35 minutes

1 pint strawberries, washed and quartered
1 pint raspberries, rinsed and patted dry
1 pint blackberries or blueberries, rinsed and patted dry
juice of one lemon
2 tsp. arrowroot (or cornstarch)
1 oz. fructose
6 oz. barley malt

1 cup granola, plain or with dried fruit
½ cup oat flour
½ tsp. sea salt
½ tsp. chopped walnuts
4 tbsp. whole sunflower seeds
dash nutmeg and cinnamon
frozen yogurt or non-dairy topping (optional)

1. Preheat oven to 375 degrees.

2. Mix together berries, lemon juice, arrowroot, fructose, and 3 ounces of the barley malt. Reserve.

3. In a separate bowl, comine and mix together granola, flour, salt, walnuts, sunflower seeds, nutmeg, cinnamon, and remaining barley malt. Set aside.

4. In an oven-proof dish, place the berry mixture and top with granola mixture, spreading it evenly over the surface of the fruit. Bake in preheated oven for 30 to 35 minutes, until the topping is golden and the fruit is cooked through and bubbling.

5. Serve with nonfat vanilla frozen yogurt or a calorie-reduced non-dairy topping.

ONE SERVING: 497 Calories; 32.7 grams Fat (4.4 Saturated); 0 mg Cholesterol.

NOTE: Barley malt is a sweetener that is often sold in one-pound bags in health food stores. One gram contains three calories. Fructose is a naturally occurring sweetener. It can be purchased at health food stores in powder or liquid form.

HEALTH TIP: This dessert of fruit, nuts, and whole grains packs an admirable 11.8 grams of good-for-you fiber!

HINT: A pointed, serrated grapefruit spoon is useful for coring the pears.

If Admiral Oliver Hazard Perry had lived today instead of during the War of 1812 he might have changed his famous remark to: "We have met the enemy, and it is cholesterol!" That is, if he frequently indulged in his favorite dessert. After a hard day of battling, he looked forward to "four pounds flour, four pounds currants, four pounds butter, four pounds sugar, four pounds citron, one half an ounce mace, one half pint brandy, forty eggs. Will make a devilish good . . . cake such as I had!"

PEARS POACHED IN WHITE WINE WITH RASPBERRY SAUCE

Penelope's in Tucson specializes in the French cuisine of Chef Patricia Sparks. These spiced pears glazed with fruit would make a lovely finale to any meal.

6 Servings
Preparation Time: 15 minutes
Cooking Time: 30 minutes
Chilling Time: At least one hour

6 pears	**1½ cups raspberries,**
1 cup white wine	**fresh or frozen**
4 cups water	**without sugar**
1 tsp. ground cinnamon	**1 tbsp. Grand Marnier**
½ tsp. ground nutmeg	**(optional)**
½ tsp. ground cloves	**sugar or sweetener**
	(optional)

1. Peel and core pears (see *HINT*) from the bottom so fruit remains in one piece. Slice a thin piece off of the bottom, so each pear will stand upright.

2. In a large saucepan, bring wine, water, cinnamon, nutmeg, and cloves to a boil, whisking in spices to blend. Add peeled pears and simmer for 20 to 30 minutes, or until pears are tender. Chill pears in poaching liquid.

3. Purée berries in food processor or blender with 3 tablespoons of poaching liquid. Stir in Grand Marnier and sweetener to taste, if desired. If sauce is too thick, thin with poaching liquid, one tablespoon at a time.

4. Place pears on a serving plate. Spoon sauce over each pear; it will coat the sides of the pear and drizzle onto the plate making a puddle of sauce around the pear.

ONE SERVING (Without sugar): 113 Calories; 0.8 grams Fat; 0 mg Cholesterol.

MANGO MOUSSE

From the repertoire of Chef Robert Maxwell, who for many years delighted restaurant-goers along Longboat Key in Sarasota, Florida, comes this delectable dessert.

6 Servings
Preparation Time: 25 minutes
Chilling Time: At least 4 hours

3 cups peeled, seeded, and cubed fresh mango
1 tbsp. unflavored gelatin
¼ cup hot water
¼ cup lime juice

½ cup sugar
2 egg whites
¼ cup half-and-half
thin slices of lime
mint sprigs

1. In a blender or food processor, blend mango into a smooth purée.

2. Dissolve the gelatin in the hot water and let stand until cooled.

3. Blend the mango purée with the lime juice, stir in the sugar, and mix well. Add gelatin.

4. Beat the egg whites until frothy. Whip the half-and-half, fold it into the egg whites, then fold into the purée, gently but thoroughly.

5. Pour into individual stemmed glasses or a glass serving bowl. Refrigerate until set, at least 4 hours. Garnish with lime slices and mint.

ONE SERVING: 150 Calories; 2.0 grams Fat; 5 mg Cholesterol.

HEALTH TIP: Full of vitamins, mangoes are the darling of nutritionists as well as chefs. They have been called the "peach of the tropics." In fact, peaches make an acceptable substitute if mangoes are unavailable.

NOTE: In your quest for the best mango, seek a ripe fruit that is slightly soft and very aromatic. This is a better gauge than the skin color, which can range anywhere from green to yellow to red, depending on ripeness and/or the variety of mango.

Index

110-11; Herb-Crusted Codfish in Rosemary Vinaigrette, 95-96; Mahimahi Oporto, 113; Monkfish Medallions with Asparagus, Morels, and Madeira, 103; nutritional benefits of, 97, 123; Pan-Seared Swordfish with Toasted Rice Sauce, 108-9; Pan-Seared Tuna Steak with Lobster and Fresh Fennel Sauce, 98; Poached Salmon with Dilled Cucumber Sauce, 105; Portuguese Swordfish, 102; Red Snapper with Golden Tomato Salsa, 99; Roasted Smoked Halibut with Braised Cabbage and Parsleyed Potatoes, 100-101; Roasted Swordfish with Olives and Leeks, 97; Salmon with Tomato and Chives, 106; Swordfish in Mustard Seed Crust, 124; Tuna Decatur, 117-18

Floating Island on Strawberry Purée with Kiwi, 193

Florida Oysters Rockefeller, 22

Four Seasons (Philadelphia), 30, 33, 42, 59, 72, 88, 199

French Laundry (Napa Valley, California), 46, 194

Fructose, 197

Fruit, health benefits of, 198, 199

Fruit concentrate, 162, 191

Garden salad with smoked tomato dressing, 70

Garlic: Garlic-Chive Oil, 101; Garlic, Lemon, Olive, and Mint Compote, 169; Roasted Elephant Garlic, 157-58; Opryland Garlic Dressing, 65-66; Roasted Garlic, 186-87

Ginger, how to peel, 85

Gloria's Black Bean Soup, 49-50

Golden Gazpacho with Bay Scallops, 52-53

Grilled Beef with Horseradish Sauce (variation), 158-59

Grilled Chicken with Honey, Lime, and Garlic Glaze, 148

Grilled Chicken with Salad and Fresh Herbs, 142

Grilled Chicken with Tomato-Pepper Salsa, 128-29

Grilled Lobster and Scallop Kebobs, 120

Grilled Marinated Vegetable Cobb Salad, 60-61

Grilled Salmon with Fresh Corn and Tomato Salsa, 107

Grilled Shrimp with Artichokes, Fettucine, and Roasted Radicchio Vinaigrette, 29-30

Grilled Tuna on Roasted Vegetables with Pineapple-Soy Vinaigrette, 110-11

Gypsy Cab Company (St. Augustine, Florida), 107

Halekulani Hotel (Oahu, Hawaii), 69

Halibut: Broiled Fillet of Pacific Halibut with Cilantro-Artichoke Relish, 114; Marinated Halibut Salad, 68; Roasted Smoked Halibut, 100-101

Hamersley's Bistro (Boston), 116, 152, 168, 169

Hawaiian Sorbet, 198

Hedgerose Heights Inn (Atlanta), 28

Herbs: bouquet garni, 141, 158; Herb Broth, 87-88; Herb-Crusted Codfish, 95-96; Herbes de Provence, 152, 182; Grilled Chicken with Salad and Fresh Herbs, 142; use of fresh and dried, 120

Horseradish crust for fish, 112-13

Hunt Club (Seattle), 157

Iberian (Huntington, New York), 145

Il Gattopardo (New York City), 77

Italian fare: Angel Hair Pasta with Chicken, Basil, and Olives, 80; Cappellini with Grilled Swordfish, Baby Vegetables, and Herb Broth, 87-88; Christmas Italian Rice Pudding, 195; Pasta Primavera, 77; Pasta with Sundried and Fresh Tomato Sauce, 82-83; Pizza Provençal, 30-31; Red Pepper Pesto, 79; Stonehill chicken, 131-32; Ziti Italiano, 86

Ivy's (San Francisco), 144, 186

Janos (Tucson), 25, 40, 122

Jicama, 52

Jody's Fire and Ice Tomatoes, 72

Joe's (San Francisco), 153

Joe's Greek Special, 153-54

John Clancy's (New York City), 103

Kahala Hilton (Honolulu, Hawaii), 91, 158

Kale: nutritional value, 116; purchasing and storing, 116

Key Lime Linguine with Crab and Mustard Sauce, 78

King Cole (Dayton, Ohio), 84, 154, 175, 180, 188

Kiwi, 193

Lafitte's Landing (Donaldsonville, Louisiana), 21, 104, 121, 174

Lamb: calorie content, 160; Garlic, Lemon and Mint Compote for, 169; Grilled Lamb, 160-61; Lamb Spirals with Pine Nuts and Garlic, 167; Spiced Lamb Shanks with Eggplant, 152-53; wine to accompany, 160

Lark and The Dove (Atlanta), 143

La Tour (Chicago), 26, 29

L'Auberge (Dayton, Ohio), 64, 127

Le Bernardin (New York City), 51, 95

Le Dome (Ft. Lauderdale), 72

Leeks: Roasted Swordfish with Olives and Leeks, 97

Lemon-Basil Oil, 101

Lemongrass, purchasing, 51

Lemon Pepper Chicken, 137

Lentil, Red Pepper, and Onion Sauté, 175

Le Supreme de Poulet a la Provençale, 141

Lobster and Scallop Kebobs, 120

Lucy Chu's Poached Chicken, 129

Madeleines: Chocolate Madeleines, 196; history of, 196

Mahimahi Oporto, 113

Maisonette (Cincinnati, Ohio), 135, 166, 193

Mango Mousse, 202

Mansion on Turtle Creek (Dallas), 108, 178

Marinated Halibut Salad, 68

Meat: See Beef, Lamb, Pork, Veal, or Venison

Melon: Champagne Melon Soup, 47

Mexican fare: Chico's Chili, 165; Enchiladas Verdes, 139-40; nutritional components, 183; Winter Tomato Soup with Oregano and Orange, 46-47; Zocalo Black Beans, 183

Milk: evaporated skim, 43, 78, 195

Miso, 90